Cause

RECONSTRUCTION AMERICA, 1863–1877

TONYA BOLDEN

ALFRED A. KNOPF
NEW YORK

THIS IS A BORZOI BOOK PUBLISHED BY ALFRED A. KNOPF

Text copyright © 2005 by Tonya Bolden

Illustration credits can be found on page 131.

www.randomhouse.com/kids

Library of Congress Cataloging-in-Publication Data
Bolden, Tonya.
Cause : Reconstruction America, 1863–1877 / Tonya Bolden. — 1st ed.
p.   cm.
ISBN 0-375-82795-1 (trade) — ISBN 0-375-92795-6 (lib. bdg.)
1. Reconstruction (U.S. history, 1865–1877)—Juvenile literature.
2. United States—History—1865–1898—Juvenile literature. I. Title.
E668.B674   2005
973.7'1—dc22   2005018138

Printed in the United States of America
December 2005
10 9 8 7 6 5 4 3 2 1
First Edition

For my Southern forebears, who persevered up from slavery, and in so doing, caused me to be

—T.B.

CONTENTS

Prologue 1

CHAPTER *1*
"Traitors Must Be Punished" .4

CHAPTER *2*
"To a Fairer Future of Liberty and Peace" 8

CHAPTER *3*
"Johnson, We Have Faith in You" 14

CHAPTER *4*
"This Is a Country for White Men" 21

CHAPTER *5*
"A Blow to Our Government System" 28

CHAPTER *6*
"We Are Americans" 33

CHAPTER *7*
"Cause" 39

CHAPTER *8*
"Why Not Hang Thad Stevens!" 44

CHAPTER *9*
"Making a Whipping-Post of the South" 49

CHAPTER *10*
"We Are Wise Enough" 54

CHAPTER *11*
"The Great Obstruction" 59

CHAPTER *12*
"Or Other High Crimes and Misdemeanors" 64

CHAPTER *13*
"The Bill Do Pass" 70

CHAPTER *14*
"Let Us Have Peace" 75

CHAPTER *15*
"On Account of Race, Color, or Previous Condition of Servitude" 79

CHAPTER *16*
"We Are Governing the South Too Much" 85

CHAPTER *17*
"All We Want Is to Live Under the Law" 91

CHAPTER *18*
"Why Is This, Ma?" 97

CHAPTER *19*
"The Promises in Your Constitution" 104

CHAPTER *20*
"A Doubtful Election" 111

Epilogue 118

Notes 123

Selected Sources 129

Illustration Credits 131

Acknowledgments 132

Index 133

PROLOGUE

Dead Confederate forces from the Battle of Antietam (also known as Sharpsburg) in Maryland. It was the bloodiest single day of the war (September 17, 1862). Each side suffered more than ten thousand casualties.

The Civil War is hands down the most captivating period in American history. More than sixty thousand books have been published on the subject. The nation's reunion—Reconstruction—is no less deserving of our attention.

Reconstruction was a time of recovery: a nation torn asunder becoming one again. But should the failed breakaway states be treated as if nothing had happened? People, North and South, were also wrapping their minds around the reality that chattel slavery would be no more—nowhere—in America. And what then? Should the federal government reimburse slaveholders for their liberated human holdings? Would freed people be compensated for those bitter years of stolen labor, brutality, and attempted soul murder? If so, by whom? The federal government? The people who had held them in bondage?

Beaufort, South Carolina, 1862. When Union forces triumphed in the area, planters fled. Their confiscated property included about ten thousand black people. The U.S. government recruited reform-minded Northerners to go to the area to educate and in other ways help these people transition from slavery to liberty and prove to doubting whites that freed people could handle freedom. These initiatives are known as "dress rehearsals" for Reconstruction.

Charleston, South Carolina, in 1865, four years after the Civil War began there.

Were once-enslaved and never-enslaved "coloreds" or "negroes" really to be Americans?

A few years before the war, in the *Dred Scott* case, the U.S. Supreme Court ruled that blacks never were, never could be, and never should be citizens. Chief Justice Roger Taney insisted that the fifty-five white men who crafted the Constitution, the ultimate law of the land, had put the nation—the world—on notice that blacks "had no rights which the white man was bound to respect." After the war, the nation convulsed with calls for and against black men having the same rights as white men.

What about the rights of women? What about Native Americans in a nation steadily expanding its turf? Reconstruction was a riptide of issues. *Cause: Reconstruction America, 1863–1877* is an overview and gateway to more in-depth study of this tempestuous era.

"TRAITORS MUST BE PUNISHED"

Andrew Johnson, born dirt poor in Raleigh, North Carolina. He never had the benefit of formal schooling because his hometown had no public school. While children of the wealthy in the area frolicked, young Johnson, like his older brother William, served as an apprentice to a local tailor.

Vice President Andy Johnson was asleep on the night of April 14, 1865, when urgent knocks rocked the door of his rooms at Kirkwood House, the Washington, D.C., hotel that was his home away from home. Behind the door, horrible news: President Lincoln—shot. With his wife and another couple, the president had been enjoying a comedy at D.C.'s Ford's Theatre when John Wilkes Booth pulled the trigger.

The shooting of the president wasn't the night's only tragedy. Armed with a pistol and bowie knife, a hulk of a man invaded Secretary of State William Seward's home, stabbed him repeatedly as he lay in bed, then cycloned back out into the night.

Rumors ricocheted around D.C. that several higher-ups in Lincoln's administration had been slain—including the very much alive Andy Johnson. He had rushed to Lincoln's side, then returned to Kirkwood House, where he paced, where he pledged, "They shall suffer for this. They shall suffer for this," and where he, no doubt, pondered the possible—the probable—impact of Booth's bullet on *his* life.

Stubborn, combative, shrewd, and sometimes crude, Andy Johnson was a tailor by trade. He had opened his own shop in the East Tennessee town of Greeneville, where he had a farm and other property, including about a half dozen black people. As he powered up economically, he scratched his political itch.

Quick at the lip and a strong debater, Johnson entered politics as an alderman in the late 1820s and went on to become Greeneville's mayor. Like most white Southerners, Johnson was a die-hard Democrat. That party's battle cry was "states' rights." Democrats believed that states should have the final say in their affairs, from who could vote to whether to abolish slavery. For them, the Tenth Amendment was the jewel in the Constitution's crown. It said that any powers not given to the federal government and not forbidden to the states "are reserved to the States respectively, or to the people."

After his term as mayor, Johnson served eight years in the Tennessee legislature, then ten years in the U.S. House of Representatives. Throughout, he championed the cause of whites of humble means. "Some day I will show the stuck-up aristocrats who is running the country," he boasted. Andy Johnson hated the wealthy planters. He called them a "cheap purse-proud set" and "not half as good as the man who earns his bread by the sweat of the brow." Johnson tried to get the government to let poor whites have some public domain land to homestead at little or no cost. He beat this drum during his two terms as governor of Tennessee and throughout his time in the U.S. Senate, which he entered in the late 1850s. He held himself up as an example of what a person birthmarked as "white trash" could achieve—even become Mr. President?

Johnson's hope of being the Democratic Party's presidential candidate in 1860 ended in disappointment. So did his party's hope of winning the

Confederate president, Kentucky-born Mississippi cotton planter and slaveholder Jefferson Davis, son of a Revolutionary War veteran and a West Point graduate himself (1828). Davis had been in the military during the U.S.-Mexican War (1846–1848), through which America came into possession of California, almost all of the Southwest, and part of Wyoming (with virtually all the Mexicans living in its new lands subject to second-class citizenship). Before that war, Jeff Davis was a member of the U.S. House of Representatives; after, of the U.S. Senate; then President Franklin Pierce's secretary of war. In 1857, Davis returned to the Senate. He resigned in January 1861 after Mississippi seceded. "We feel that our cause is just and holy . . . all we ask is to be let alone," he declared a few weeks after his forces attacked Fort Sumter.

The first Confederate cabinet. Clockwise, from top: Secretary of State Robert Toombs, former U.S. representative and senator (Georgia); Secretary of War Leroy Pope Walker, former state legislator and judge (Alabama); Attorney General Judah Philip Benjamin, former U.S. senator (Louisiana), whom anti-Semites called "Davis's pet Jew"; Postmaster General John Henninger Reagan, former U.S. representative and senator (Texas); Secretary of the Navy Stephen Russell Mallory, former U.S. senator (Florida); and Secretary of the Treasury Christopher Gustavus Memminger, former state legislator (South Carolina). Center: The Virginia state capitol building. It doubled as the Confederate government seat when its capital moved from Montgomery, Alabama, to Richmond.

presidency. Its main competition was the Republican Party, dominated by Northerners, many of whom had bolted from the Democratic, Whig, and other parties. The glue holding the Republican Party together was a desire to stop the spread of slavery into western territories. The Republicans adamant about abolishing slavery *and* establishing civil rights for blacks were the "radicals."

In the November 1860 presidential election, Republicans were the victors with the lanky lawyer from Springfield, Illinois, Abe Lincoln. "I believe this government cannot endure permanently half slave and half free," he had said years earlier. Slavery was still legal in fifteen states when Lincoln won the presidency. The nation was abuzz with talk of his working to abolish it. How? When?

South Carolina decided not to stick around to find out. About a month after the election, it issued its Ordinance of Secession, announcing that "the Union now subsisting between South Carolina and other States, under the name of the United States of America, is hereby dissolved." By early February 1861, six more states had seceded. With South Carolina, they formed a new nation: the Confederate States of America (CSA); its president, Jeff Davis of Mississippi.

On April 12, 1861, CSA forces fired on the U.S.-manned Fort Sumter in South Carolina's Charleston Harbor. It was the tripwire of war!—"The War of Northern Aggression," "The War Between the States," "The War for Abolition," "The War of Southern Independence," "The War to Save the Union," "The Second American Revolution." It was the eighty-five-year-old nation's civil war. Before spring was out, four more states joined the CSA, Andy Johnson's Tennessee among them.

Tennessee had a sizeable population longing to stay loyal to the Union, and Johnson was at the forefront of the movement—the only U.S. senator from a CSA state who did not resign his seat. He believed one right a state did

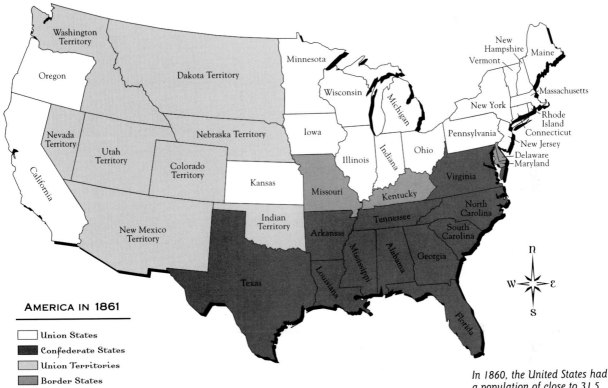

AMERICA IN 1861

☐ Union States
■ Confederate States
▨ Union Territories
▨ Border States

In 1860, the United States had a population of close to 31.5 million. Of the roughly 4 million blacks enslaved, about 3.5 million lived in what became the CSA. There were fewer than fifty people enslaved in the West. The rest were in the Border States, which did not join the CSA, and the nation's capital. Slavery was abolished in the territories and D.C. in 1862. Pro-Union sentiments in Virginia's northwestern counties resulted in a new state, West Virginia (1863). Indian Territory came about from the federal government's fervor to remove as many Native Americans as possible from the Southeast in the early 1800s. The land set aside for and governed by native peoples was originally much larger. At one point, it included Kansas and Nebraska. In the early twentieth century, Indian Territory ceased to exist. It became Oklahoma.

not have was the right to secede, and he agreed with most Northerners that secessionists had committed treason. "Treason must be made odious, and traitors must be punished and impoverished," he often declared. As for traitorous aristocrats, "Their great plantations must be seized and divided into small farms, and sold to honest, industrious men." Jeff Davis and other high-ranking Confederates "ought to be hung." Confederates cursed Johnson; Unionists showered him with praise.

After Union forces gained significant control of Tennessee, President Lincoln made Andy Johnson the state's military governor, in March 1862. Johnson presided over the firing and jailing of officeholders who did not swear allegiance to the United States. He put the kibosh on anti-Union newspapers. He schemed with army officers on how to keep the state from CSA conquest. One big worry was the cavalry brigade led by Tennessee-born Nathan Bedford Forrest, a wealthy slaveholding cotton planter. Nothing would give Forrest more pleasure than to get Andy Johnson in his clutches.

2

"TO A FAIRER FUTURE OF LIBERTY AND PEACE"

Abraham Lincoln, born poor in Kentucky, and self-taught. His early political career included a stint in the legislature of his adopted home state, Illinois, and one term in the U.S. House of Representatives. Though Lincoln understood that slavery was wrong, he did not always cotton to blacks remaining in America. Early on in the war, he lobbied for government-financed resettlement of blacks, with West Africa and Central America among the places considered. The Emancipation Proclamation did not apply to the roughly 800,000 blacks enslaved in the Border States and in Union-occupied Tennessee and parts of Louisiana and Virginia, in order to keep these places loyal. The proclamation was, as Lincoln stated, a "war measure."

President Abraham Lincoln would make the ultimate Confederate trophy—he who was responsible for the Union's confiscation of Confederate property where Union forces conquered, he who was responsible for a proclamation that created more chaos on the CSA home front and bedeviled its war effort: the Emancipation Proclamation. It decreed that as of January 1, 1863, the roughly three million children and adults enslaved in CSA-controlled

Lincoln's Emancipation Proclamation technically did not free anyone, but it had a profound psychological effect, especially on enslaved people who got wind of it: thousands headed for Union lines. Those who stayed with the troops worked for their keep, if able-bodied, as laundresses, cooks, laborers, and scouts. About half of the roughly one hundred and eighty thousand black men who served in the Union Army came from CSA states. This engraving of a moment of jubilee on a road to New Bern, North Carolina, in late January 1863, ran in the February 21, 1863, issue of **Harper's Weekly**. The newspaper, subtitled "A Journal of Civilization," was nineteenth-century America's leading illustrated newspaper.

territory would be "forever free." On top of that, black men could join the Union Army, which would be a segregated army.

In December 1863, Lincoln announced another initiative to weaken the CSA: his Proclamation of Amnesty and Reconstruction. It promised to pardon rebels who pledged allegiance to the United States and acceptance of the abolition of slavery. Exceptions included people who held top posts in the CSA government and armed forces; people who had quit the U.S. courts, Congress, or the armed forces in support of the CSA; and CSA soldiers who had abused black prisoners of war and their white officers.

If at least 10 percent of a state's citizens who had the right to vote before the war (white men over the age of twenty-one) took the oath, that state could establish a new state government loyal to the Union. Andy Johnson supported Lincoln's "Ten Percent Plan." Not that Johnson had come to see that slavery was immoral. He firmly believed blacks should be nothing more than property. But if preserving the Union meant losing slavery, so be it. He was in a "war for the Constitution and the Union."

Andy Johnson's loyalty to the Union paid off big when Lincoln geared up to run for reelection in 1864. Republicans hoped to woo Democrats by having one on the ticket. Johnson replaced radical-leaning Vice President Hannibal Hamlin as Lincoln's running mate. Forbidding slavery in all states that were and would ever be part of America was a keynote campaign issue. Congress had in the works an amendment to the Constitution that would do just that. Lincoln

General William Tecumseh Sherman, "Cump" to family and friends. His father named him "Tecumseh" after the legendary Shawnee warrior-chief. Like his good friend General Ulysses S. Grant, Sherman was a native of Ohio, a West Point graduate (1840), and a veteran of the U.S.-Mexican War. In early 1865, Sherman issued Special Field Order No. 15. It set aside, for blacks, certain lands abandoned by whites: a strip of land from coastal Charleston, South Carolina, to Jacksonville, Florida, along with Edisto, St. Simon, and other Sea Islands. Sherman issued the order at Secretary of War Edwin Stanton's prompting and was happy to oblige because he wanted to liberate his troops from the throngs of blacks who clung to them.

urged Congress to pass this thirteenth amendment.

Being in league with Lincoln made Andy Johnson all the more anathema to Confederates. *Traitor!* they called him all the louder, especially after his speech before a crowd of blacks in Nashville, on the steps of the state capitol building in late October 1864. Acknowledging that blacks had suffered "a storm of persecution," Johnson wished them "a Moses" to lead them to a "promised land of freedom and happiness."

"You are our Moses!" blacks hurrahed, no doubt thinking him a changed man.

Johnson assured the crowd that God had someone in mind to do a "great work" for them, saying that "in due time your leader will come forth, your Moses will be revealed to you."

"We want no Moses but you!"

"If no other better shall be found, I will indeed be your Moses," responded Johnson. Just as the Old Testament patriarch brought Hebrews out of Egyptian slavery, he said he would lead blacks "through the Red Sea of war and bondage to a fairer future of liberty and peace."

No matter what Johnson promised blacks or anyone else, the thought of him as vice president rankled some Republicans. "Can't you get a candidate for Vice-President without going down into a damned rebel province for one?" radical Thad Stevens had asked an advisor to Lincoln. The caustic, clubfooted Stevens, a U.S. representative for Pennsylvania, had told the president what he thought of Johnson: "a damn scoundrel," among other things.

With Union general Sheridan's devastation of Virginia's Shenandoah Valley and General Sherman's rampage in Georgia in fall 1864, Northern morale soared, as did the popularity of the Republican Party, by then calling itself the National Union Party for patriotic effect. The Lincoln-Johnson ticket triumphed over the Northern Democratic Party's ticket (General George McClellan and George Pendleton). Come inauguration day, March 4, 1865, after Lincoln and Johnson took the oaths of office in the Capitol Building, Thad

Stevens would have to deal with addressing the "damn scoundrel" as "Mr. Vice President."

Johnson's arriving at the inauguration liquored up made him even more suspect. Everyone was mortified. (Johnson was ill and thought a little whiskey would give him vigor, but then a little became more and more.) But a tipsy Johnson wasn't the most troubling thing for renowned abolitionist Fred Douglass, who attended the inauguration and the party that followed at the Executive Mansion, the official name of the White House back then. As Douglass chatted with an acquaintance, President Lincoln pointed him out to Johnson. Fred Douglass never forgot the look on Johnson's face—"one of bitter contempt and aversion." Then: "Seeing that I observed him, he tried to assume a more friendly appearance, but it was too late." Unlike blacks who had cheered Johnson in Nashville, Douglass saw in him no Moses. "Whatever Andrew Johnson may be," he said to his acquaintance, "he certainly is no friend of our race."

Neither was Confederate loyalist John Wilkes Booth. He had loathed Lincoln's Emancipation Proclamation. He had fumed when Congress passed the Thirteenth Amendment in January 1865. A few months later came greater devastations for Booth and like-minded folk. On April 7, Richmond, Virginia, the CSA capital, fell to Union troops. Two days later, Palm Sunday, in the courthouse of the Virginia village of Appomattox, the CSA's most celebrated general, Robert E. Lee, surrendered to the Union general with the winning nation's initials in his name: U. S. Grant. The Civil War was essentially over.

On April 11, 1865, Abe Lincoln gave a speech from the balcony of the

Peter Lloyd was among the thousands of blacks who took advantage of General Sherman's Special Field Order No. 15. General Rufus Saxton was in charge of land distribution: each household could have no more than forty acres. At some point, the army decided to give people some surplus mules. Hope twinned with misinformation led to the belief that the federal government had promised all freed people "forty acres and a mule."

Hiram Ulysses Grant became "Ulysses Simpson Grant" due to a clerical error when he entered West Point. After he left the army in 1854, Grant failed miserably at farming and other endeavors before he became a clerk at his family's leather-goods store in Galena, Illinois. Hungry for a commission when the Civil War broke out, he became colonel of the rambunctious 21st Illinois Volunteers. Like Andy Johnson, Grant was dogged by talk that he was a drunkard, but his bravery and largely brilliant battle plans earned him President Lincoln's praise and a promotion to general-in-chief of the Union Army in March 1864. At war's end, General Grant was hoorayed as the "Hero of Appomattox." He was a man of few words, except around intimates or when riled.

*Like his famous father and two of his brothers, Maryland-born John Wilkes Booth was an actor—very dramatic, very physical, and prone to entering a scene with a leap from on high. A few weeks before he shot President Lincoln, Booth starred at Ford's Theatre in **The Apostate**. The play climaxes with the murder of a tyrant.*

Executive Mansion. The recent victories "give hope of a righteous and speedy peace," he told the crowd with the mercurial John Wilkes Booth in its midst. Along with rejoicing, there was work to do, the president reminded the people. He said that the "re-inauguration of the national authority—reconstruction" was "pressed much more closely upon our attention." He warned that the process was "fraught with great difficulty." He then revisited his Ten Percent Plan and talked about how Louisiana had followed through satisfactorily. Its lawmakers had the power to grant black male suffrage (the right to vote, which no women had). The president hoped they would exercise that power soon—but heeding his preference that they limit the vote to black men who were "very intelligent" and those who had served in the U.S. armed forces.

The idea of *any* black man voting enraged John Wilkes Booth. "That means nigger citizenship," he muttered to a companion. As for Lincoln, Booth vowed to kill him. Three days later, Good Friday, 1865, armed with a single-shot .44-caliber pistol, Booth snuck up behind Lincoln in the presidential box at Ford's Theatre and shot him in the head. Booth let loose some Latin—"*Sic semper tyrannis!*" ("Thus always to tyrants!")—then bounded over the box and down onto the stage some twelve feet below, where he issued a proclamation of his own—"The South shall be free!" He dashed backstage, then out into the alley where a clueless stagehand held the reins of a getaway horse.

A manhunt was under way as physicians did all they could for Lincoln, who lay dying in a boardinghouse near the theater, and as Andy Johnson raged back at his hotel. A little after seven o'clock the next morning, Lincoln died. A few hours later, in a private ceremony at Kirkwood House, Andy Johnson was sworn in as the nation's seventeenth president. It fell upon him to pick up where Wartime Reconstruction left off, in a nation that was an absolute mess.

Thirteenth Amendment

Section 1. Neither slavery nor involuntary servitude, except as a punishment for crime whereof the party shall have been duly convicted, shall exist within the United States, or any place subject to their jurisdiction.

Section 2. Congress shall have power to enforce this article by appropriate legislation.

For the Thirteenth Amendment to become part of the Constitution, the legislatures of at least three-fourths of the states (twenty-seven of thirty-six) needed to ratify it. The count was twenty-one the day President Lincoln died, April 15, 1865.

In allowing for slavery as punishment for a crime, the Thirteenth Amendment upheld prison slave labor, a tradition inherited from Britain.

"JOHNSON, WE HAVE FAITH IN YOU"

"The stench from the dead between our line and theirs was . . . so nauseating that it was almost unendurable," recalled CSA colonel William Oates of the June 1864 Battle of Cold Harbor, Virginia. "The dead covered more than five acres of ground." In this April 1865 photograph of some of that ground, a labor detail gathers remains of Union soldiers for proper burial.

More than fourteen hundred days of war. More than six hundred thousand military and civilian deaths, from revolver, rifle, and cannon shot, from sword and saber slashes, from starvation in sieges, from disease. As for the battle-scarred and mind-marred, no one knows the count.

And several million black people were getting a grip on liberty. Most were homeless, moneyless, and illiterate. Many were enduring the agony of family—brother, sister, husband, wife, children—sold away before the war and perhaps lost to them forever. Many had lost pieces of themselves—ear, finger, half a foot, a smooth back—punishment for not working fast enough, hard enough, for having tried to escape.

America reeked of hatred. So many blacks hated whites for generations of slavery. So many whites, former slaveholders and not, hated blacks for asserting their equal humanity. Pro-Confederate Southerners hated fellow Southerners who had supported the Union as much as they hated the Yankees who carved their names, their regiments, in Southern trees; accosted Southern belles; raided and ransacked Southern mansions and hovels; stole Southern silver, livestock, and fowl; and torched Southern fields.

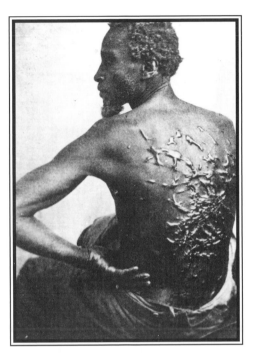

Barefoot, ragged, and carrying the scars of a flogging in Mississippi on Christmas Day, 1862, this man, known as "Gordon," reached Union forces in Baton Rouge, Louisiana, in March 1863—reporting for duty. After medical attention, food, and rest, he became a soldier. At war's end, many white Southerners feared that people like Gordon would seek bloody revenge against their former "masters."

From the May 19, 1866, issue of **Harper's Weekly**: *soldiers reunite with loved ones in Little Rock, Arkansas, in April 1865. For years after the war, black newspapers carried streams of "information wanted" ads, like the one Emeline Hodges of Leavenworth, Kansas, placed in the* **Christian Recorder** *in 1870. She was looking for her father— "Jerry Hodges, of Norfolk County, Va. I was sold from him when a small girl, about 30 years ago"—and her mother— "My mother's name was Phebe, and she belonged to a man named Ashcroth."*

The ruins of a depot in Atlanta, Georgia, courtesy of Cump, a true believer in "total war." After he sacked Atlanta in fall 1864, General Sherman commenced his famous/infamous four-hundred-mile "March to the Sea" to Savannah, with roughly one hundred thousand troops to do his bidding. They torched, shot up, blew up, or hauled off just about everything that could be of use to the Confederacy, from livestock to railroad tracks.

Many Yankees hated "Copperheads" (Northern Democrats who were antiwar and may have rooted for the CSA), and some Yankees wanted to punish—humiliate—*shame* the South—make it *pay* for Union troops massacred when they surrendered, *pay* for abusing Union prisoners of war, *pay* for celebrating Abe Lincoln's death, *pay* for catapulting the nation into the fourteen hundred days of war.

And so many Southerners were still so rebellious, including ones from non-CSA states. "I am for Jeff Davis," a woman in Louisville, Kentucky, habitually yelled out, reported a mid-May 1865 issue of the *New York Times*. "I am for Jeff Davis until my last breath is out of my body. You may stick a bayonet through my heart, and I'll be for Jeff Davis." This woman was evidence that "some rebel 'shes' continue defiant," like many rebel hes. Authorities had jailed the woman for her declarations of loyalty to the CSA's president. Davis had been captured in Georgia on May 10, then imprisoned in Virginia's Fort Monroe to await trial for treason. If found guilty, he would be hanged.

Many Republicans applauded jailing the likes of that Louisville rebel "she." They definitely celebrated the capture of Jeff Davis. And the radicals couldn't wait for Andy Johnson to teach the rebel states a lesson, given his frequent declaration that traitors must be punished.

"Johnson, we have faith in you," Ohio senator Ben Wade had declared in a meeting with the president on the day he was sworn in. "By the gods, there will be no trouble now in running the government." Wade hated Lincoln's reconstruction plan—*too lenient!* Secretary of War Edwin Stanton, who had been tight with Lincoln, agreed.

One of the first things Johnson had to deal with was the plot that caused him to be president. (Secretary of State Seward, who was recovering from a carriage accident when stabbed, survived.) Booth and an accomplice had been tracked down in late April, holed up in a barn near Port Royal, Virginia. A zealous sergeant had availed himself of an opening in the barn wall and shot Booth. His death put a monkey wrench in the investigation. Like the secretary of war and others, President Johnson strongly suspected that the plot's grand master wasn't Booth but rather Jeff Davis. Proof was elusive, but in the search, hundreds of people were rounded up and thrown in jail. After the whirlwind, eight "conspirators" faced a military tribunal. Four of them ended up in prison; four swung from a rope.

By then President Johnson had revealed his plan for the rebels in general. In late May 1865, while Congress was not in session, he issued two proclamations.

*From the September 16, 1865, issue of **Harper's Weekly**: scenes from Camp Sumter, the Confederacy's most notorious prisoner-of-war camp, commonly called Andersonville after a nearby southwestern Georgia town. Built to hold about ten thousand prisoners, the camp saw that number triple, with one-third dying. The camp's commandant, Hartmann Heinrich "Henry" Wirz, a Swiss émigré, was tried and found guilty of war crimes, then hanged in November 1865, in the courtyard of Old Capitol Prison, across the street from the Capitol Building. Many Northerners relished Wirz's execution because they believed the Andersonville horrors were intentional. But according to **The Library of Congress Civil War Desk Reference**, historians "generally agree that the enormous suffering at Andersonville resulted from an inept bureaucracy, limited resources, and a severely disrupted infrastructure, rather than deliberate cruelty."*

*This engraving from the June 3, 1865, issue of **Harper's Weekly**, captioned "RICHMOND LADIES GOING TO RECEIVE GOVERNMENT RATIONS," has one "rebel she" saying to the other: "Don't you think that Yankee must feel like shrinking into his boots before such high-toned Southern ladies as we!" The artist left it up to viewers to imagine the cause of the black woman's smile.*

*Ohio's Benjamin Franklin Wade, former prosecuting attorney, state senator, and judge, who entered the U.S. Senate in 1851. In the summer of 1864, Wade and Representative Henry Winter Davis (Maryland) co-authored a bill with a tougher requirement for a rebel state's readmission (at least 51 percent of its white men had to pledge loyalty). Both houses of Congress passed the bill, but Lincoln rejected it. Wade and Davis went ballistic. "Our support is of a cause and not of a man," they declared in their manifesto, which ran in an August 1864 issue of the **New York Tribune**. They insisted that "the authority of Congress is paramount and must be respected." If Lincoln wanted their support, he had better "leave political reorganization to Congress."*

The first was his "Proclamation of Amnesty." Its terms for pardon were about the same as Lincoln's, except that confiscated land could not be returned and its list of people ineligible for amnesty was longer. It included the people who came to be called the "$20,000 men": rebels with taxable property (such as real estate) valued at more than $20,000 (roughly $22 million today). A personal appeal to Andy Johnson was their only hope for pardon.

In his second proclamation, known as the "North Carolina Proclamation," Johnson named Democrat William Holden provisional governor of North Carolina.

"EXECUTION OF THE CONSPIRATORS—ADJUSTING THE ROPE," from the July 22, 1865, issue of **Harper's Weekly**. The four people sentenced to death for co-conspiring with Booth were hanged in the courtyard of D.C.'s Old Capitol Prison on Friday, July 7, 1865, a day of searing sun (hence the umbrellas). The four were: Lewis Powell (CSA Army veteran), who attacked Secretary of State Seward; David Herold (drugstore clerk), who was with Booth when he vowed to kill President Lincoln and when authorities caught up with him; George Atzerodt (blockade runner), who had chickened out, allegedly, on killing Andy Johnson at Kirkwood House around the same time that Booth shot Lincoln; and Mary Surratt, who ran a boardinghouse a few blocks away from Ford's Theatre. During the war, Surratt's home was a safe house for CSA spies. Allegedly, it was where much of the assassination plotting occurred. Surratt was the first woman executed by the federal government—wrongfully so, as many historians believe today, just as many people did in 1865.

The president ordered Holden to hold a convention to revise the state's constitution. Unpardoned rebels could not vote for delegates to the convention. Other than that, all prewar qualifications for voting were in effect, so still only white men could vote. North Carolina's new constitution had to repeal its ordinance of secession and ratify the Thirteenth Amendment. That done, the Tarheel State would be all right with the Union.

The North Carolina Proclamation marked the start of "Presidential Reconstruction," though Johnson took issue with the term "reconstruction."

He felt that states had no right to secede, and so the rebel states had never been out of the Union. "Their life breath has only been suspended." That was his position, prompting him on at least one occasion to proclaim, "There is no such thing as reconstruction." The radicals were troubled, restless.

By mid-July 1865, President Johnson had offered other CSA states the same deal he had offered North Carolina. He later added another condition: that the states repudiate their rebellion-related debt. That debt amounted to about $54 million that Johnson said the federal government would not be responsible for.

Many monied Northerners, from bankers and stockbrokers to owners of mills and steamboat fleets, applauded Johnson's program. It was quick. The sooner the states were restored to the Union, the sooner more business would resume, especially business revolving around cotton, the South's "white gold" and the nation's chief export. The men Johnson made temporary governors of ex-CSA states were largely on the same page as the Northern businessmen. They were in a hurry for their states to get back on their feet. Some were also in a hurry to dispel the notion that black freedom meant social and political equality with whites. Florida's governor, the New York–born William Marvin, told blacks to go back to work on the plantations where they had once slaved and "call your old Master—'Master.'" Some blacks did. Others would rather die (and some did). Still others had the nerve and wit to toy with their former "masters." These others included Jourdon Anderson.

"I thought the Yankees would have hung you long before this for harboring Rebs they found at your house," Jourdon Anderson remarked in an August 1865 letter to his former "master," Colonel P. H. Anderson of Big Spring, Tennessee. Jourdon Anderson, with his wife and children, had resettled in Ohio; somehow, the colonel had gotten a letter to him, apparently asking him to come back. "I want to know particularly what the good chance is you propose to give me," the black man asked the white man. "I served you faithfully for thirty-two years, and Mandy twenty years. At $25 a month for me, and $2 a week for Mandy, our earnings would amount to $11,680. Add to this the interest for the time our wages has been kept back and deduct what you paid for our clothing and three doctor's visits to me, and pulling a tooth for Mandy, and the balance will show what we are in justice entitled to." If the colonel didn't pay up, well then, "we can have little faith in your promises in the future." If the colonel replied, that letter has yet to be made public.

From the September 30, 1865, issue of **Harper's Weekly**: "Slabtown," so called because its one-story cottages were "built of rough barrel-staves, or slabs slit out with the axe." In 1866, about four thousand people, many supporting themselves as shoemakers, lived in this "freedmen's" village in Hampton, Virginia. There, in 1868, General Samuel Chapman Armstrong, former commander of black troops, started a school devoted to educating blacks and Native Americans. This vocational and teacher-training institute evolved into Hampton University.

Presidential Reconstruction did not spur people like Colonel Anderson to do anything for people like Jourdon Anderson. Presidential Reconstruction did not encourage whites, Northern or Southern, to treat as equals any blacks, recently freed or never enslaved. The president pointedly promoted the opposite. In speeches, correspondence, and conversation, he championed white supremacy. As he told an Upper South politician shortly after the war, "This is a country for white men, and by God, as long as I am President, it shall be a government for white men." Ben Wade could kick himself for having had faith in Johnson.

"Is there no way to arrest the insane course of the President?" complained Thad Stevens. He and other Republicans wanted the president to call Congress back into session. Congress typically adjourned before the onset of summer to avoid a stifling Capitol Building. In summer 1865, some congressmen were willing to put up with the heat because they wanted to deal with the president on Reconstruction. But Johnson didn't want to consult

Some localities in the South made it a crime for a black person not to have a job. People without proof of employment (such as a labor contract) could be charged with vagrancy, fined fifty dollars, and imprisoned if a judge so pleased. Prisoners were sometimes auctioned off or hired out to a merchant, artisan, or planter. This engraving from the January 19, 1867, issue of **Frank Leslie's Illustrated Newspaper** *carried the caption "SELLING A FREEDMAN TO PAY HIS FINE AT MONTICELLO, FLORIDA."*

with Congress, insisting that the North-South reunion was the business of the executive branch—*him*—not the legislative branch.

So, thanks to Andy Johnson, anti-black Southerners were free to keep blacks down, control their lives—especially their labor. Whites began concocting laws and customs to this end: banning blacks from renting or buying property and barring blacks from being artisans, such as carpenters and blacksmiths, so as to limit them to the lowest-paying jobs (domestic servants, field hands). Some of these "black codes" were also white codes. In Mississippi, whites who married blacks could be charged with a felony and, if convicted, "confined in the State penitentiary for life."

Freedmen's Bureau chief General Oliver Otis Howard, born in Leeds, Maine. He was a West Point graduate (1854) and a veteran of the Third Seminole War (1855–1858). A few months after he lost his right arm in the 1862 Battle of Fair Oaks, Howard was back in action. He fought in several major battles, including Antietam and Gettysburg, and commanded a wing of General Sherman's March to the Sea. The Freedmen's Bureau, established in March 1865 as a temporary agency, was part of the War Department.

Opelousas, Louisiana, created a pass system, imposed a curfew, and forbade blacks to live in the city unless they were live-in servants. South Carolina micromanaged employer-employee relations to the point of near slavery. A man who contracted to work on a plantation had to work from sunup to sundown. He also couldn't have any company or leave the plantation without permission.

To prevent blacks from being self-employed or supplementing their incomes, some places made it a crime for them to hunt and fish. Others made it illegal for them to own a gun—to keep them from hunting and from having firepower to use against whites, in particular those who patrolled black communities, many of whom were CSA Army vets. For relief from oppression and other miseries, many blacks turned to the social service agency Congress created as the war was winding down: the Bureau of Refugees, Freedmen, and Abandoned Lands. Its mission was to aid the destitute in the South, black and white. Because most of its clients were black, it became known as the Freedmen's Bureau.

Bureau offices dotted the South. Its staff set up hospitals and provided jobs for the able-bodied (construction work, for example), shelter for the homeless, for the hungry, rations—probably hardtack, salt pork, and beans—and sometimes fuel

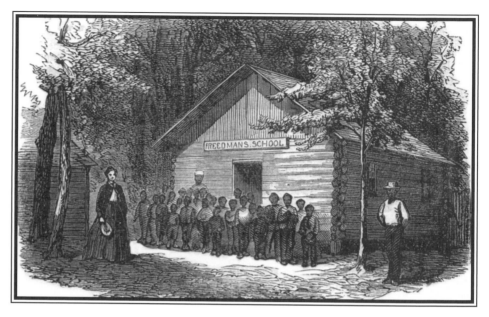

A school in North Carolina, from the October 3, 1868, issue of **Harper's Weekly**. The Freedmen's Bureau oversaw more than four thousand such schools, many of them operated by the American Missionary Association. The teachers, mostly Northerners, received little (if any) pay. Most depended on donations from churches and charitable organizations, which also sent them readers, copybooks, and other supplies. In some schools, adults were as numerous as children. "It was a whole race trying to go to school. Few were too young, and none too old, to make the attempt to learn," remembered Booker Taliaferro Washington. Born into slavery in Virginia, he was nine years old when the Civil War ended and sixteen when he entered General Armstrong's school in Hampton, sights set on being a teacher. In the early 1880s, Washington became master builder of what is now Tuskegee University in Tuskegee, Alabama.

(wood or coal) for cooking. The Freedmen's Bureau also helped many blacks realize their dream of having their own land: land in which to sow their own crop, land from which to reap and keep the whole of their harvest. The Bureau had the authority to let heads of households rent, with a later option to buy, forty-acre tracts out of the government's holdings of more than eight hundred thousand acres of abandoned or confiscated Southern land.

The Freedmen's Bureau could not help all the needy. The agency was understaffed, and some staffers were simply not up to the task. Most were soldiers. As historian W.E.B. Du Bois wrote in his study of Reconstruction, the "qualities which make a good soldier do not necessarily make a good social reformer." What's more, some whites sabotaged the Bureau's work. Agents were cursed, shot at, and shot dead. Longing to live to old age, some agents looked the other way when blacks were mistreated. Others did so for a bribe or because they thought blacks deserved to be treated like dirt.

Bad apples in the Freedmen's Bureau gave members of a black infantry regiment, the 36th, cause to write General Oliver Howard, the Bureau's chief, in spring 1865. The soldiers' families were having a terrible time on North Carolina's Roanoke Island. Their wives and children were not receiving all the rations promised when the men joined the army. It wasn't a matter of negligence or confusion but of crime: "Our ration's [sic] are stolen from the ration house." The culprits included the Bureau's assistant superintendent for black affairs on the island. What's more, white soldiers would break into black homes, "act as they please steal our chickens rob our gardens and if any one defends their-Selves against them they are taken to the gard house for it." The men of the 36th implored General Howard to rectify the situation. They ended their letter, "Signed in behalf of humanity."

The pressures and strains under which the Freedmen's Bureau operated, coupled with the fact that Presidential Reconstruction was antagonistic to black advancement, left blacks with limited options: they could resign themselves to being subservient to whites body and soul, kill themselves, become bandits, grab up pickaxes and scythes and go on murder raids, emigrate to West Africa, as close to twenty thousand blacks had done in decades past (and many whites wished they would). Or they could hope, strive, and pray. And stay in the land of their birth.

Radical Republicans were determined to help the hopeful when Congress reconvened. Things had gone from bad to worse. In late summer 1865, President Johnson had ordered the Freedmen's Bureau to return confiscated land to its original owners, who had been pardoned. Most of the blacks who now faced eviction were in the parts of South Carolina, Georgia, and Florida reserved for blacks under General Sherman's Special Field Order No. 15. Bureau chief General Oliver Howard hated having to implement Johnson's order, but not so much that he was willing to resign over it. And he certainly didn't have a pleasant time of it when he confirmed the news to blacks face to face, as he did in a meeting with Sea Islanders in October 1865.

"Why, General Howard, why do you take away our lands?" asked one of the two thousand blacks who packed a church on South Carolina's Edisto

Martin Robison Delany, born free in what is today Charles Town, West Virginia. He was a physician and newspaperman (founder of the Pittsburgh-based antislavery paper **The Mystery** and Fred Douglass's partner in the **North Star**). Convinced that blacks would never get justice in America, he advocated that blacks emigrate. (West Africa and Latin America were among the regions he considered.) Delany changed his mind about emigration after the Emancipation Proclamation. He recruited blacks for the Union Army and served himself, becoming the first black commissioned field officer. After the war, Major Delany was briefly a Freedmen's Bureau assistant commissioner in South Carolina. He was very active in Republican Party politics.

During spring and summer 1865, blacks in several states held conventions to plot out strategies for advancement. Many resulted in petitions like this one, a by-product of a meeting at the Catharine Street Baptist Church in Norfolk, Virginia, on June 5. "We do not come before the people of the United States asking an impossibility," said the Virginians, "we simply ask that a Christian and enlightened people shall, at once, concede to us the full enjoyment of those privileges of full citizenship."

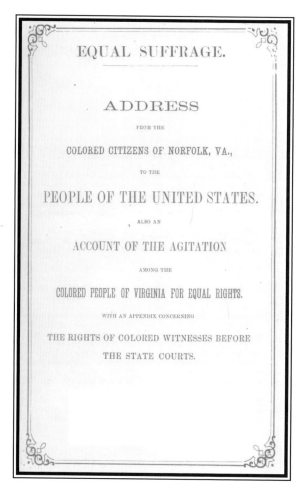

EQUAL SUFFRAGE.

ADDRESS

FROM THE

COLORED CITIZENS OF NORFOLK, VA.,

TO THE

PEOPLE OF THE UNITED STATES.

ALSO AN

ACCOUNT OF THE AGITATION

AMONG THE

COLORED PEOPLE OF VIRGINIA FOR EQUAL RIGHTS.

WITH AN APPENDIX CONCERNING

THE RIGHTS OF COLORED WITNESSES BEFORE

THE STATE COURTS.

Island. "You take them from us who are true, always true to the Government! You give them to our all-time enemies! That is not right!" Howard hoped to help the people work through the bad news—he urged them to "lay aside their bitter feelings, and to become reconciled to their old masters."

Reconciled? The Sea Islanders thought General Howard was out of his mind. "You ask us to forgive the land owners of our island. *You* only lost your right arm in war and might forgive them," said a spokesman. "The man who tied me to a tree and gave me 39 lashes and who stripped and flogged my mother and my sister and who will not let me stay in his empty hut except I will do his planting and be satisfied with his price and who combines with others to keep away land from me well knowing I would not have anything to do with him if I had land of my own—that man, I cannot well forgive."

Blacks fought to hold on to their land, by petitions and, in some cases, by not budging. But the army was forced to uphold the evictions. Exactly how many blacks had their land taken away is not known. But of the roughly forty thousand who had received about four hundred thousand acres under General Sherman's order, only about two thousand may have kept their land. Most of the others ended up working for white planters, with little choice but to be "satisfied" with their prices.

The black codes and Andy Johnson's snatching of land out of black hands were not the only developments vexing Thad Stevens and other Republicans. Johnson's soft reconstruction policy was reaping just what they feared: a stiff-necked South. Some states had not repudiated their debts. And Andy Johnson seemed okay with that. Mississippi had not ratified the Thirteenth Amendment. And Andy Johnson seemed okay with that. None of the states had given black men the right to vote. Andy Johnson was definitely okay with that. What's more, in the fall elections, waves of former CSA military and civilian officials were put into office—even into Congress. One of Georgia's newly elected congressmen was Alexander Stephens, who had declared while the CSA vice president, "Our new government . . . rests upon the great truth that the negro is not equal to the white man; that slavery—subordination to the superior race—is his natural and normal condition."

Andy Johnson was okay with men like Alexander Stephens being in Congress. The president was still a Democrat. He was still a states' rights man, and he had been doling out pardons like candy, sometimes one hundred in a single day. Thousands had gone to "$20,000 men." Johnson had become quite sympathetic toward the people he once cursed as a "purse-proud set."

By late fall 1865, the CSA states, except for Texas, had reconstituted themselves under Lincoln's or Johnson's plan. President Johnson was prepared to declare them officially restored to the Union. Republicans were not okay with that. They were poised to launch a rebellion of their own.

The U.S. Capitol Building, home of the U.S. Congress. Along with lawmaking, its powers include declaring war against and making treaties with other nations, raising taxes, and adding amendments to the Constitution. The House of Representatives (south wing) was to be the "people's house," with its members elected directly by the people every two years. For the Senate (north wing), until 1914, state legislatures did the electing (two senators, serving six-year terms, per state). December 4, 1865, marked the start of the 39th Congress. The House had 9 delegates (nonvoting representatives from the organized territories) and 193 representatives (19 from minor parties, 38 Democrats, 136 Republicans). There were 54 senators (4 from minor parties, 11 Democrats, 39 Republicans).

Article I of the Constitution states that each House of Congress "shall be the Judge of the Elections, Returns and Qualifications of its own Members." When it reconvened on Monday, December 4, 1865, the Republican-dominated Congress refused to seat recently elected senators and representatives from the former Confederacy. Congress then created a task force: nine members from the House, six from the Senate. This Joint Committee on Reconstruction was to investigate what was going on in the ex-CSA states, then advise on whether any deserved representation.

"A blow to our government system." That's what Secretary of the Navy Gideon Welles called the Republican maneuver. Welles's loyalty to President Johnson was as intense as his loathing for Secretary of War Stanton, who was allied with the radicals. As for Andy Johnson, to any and all who would listen, he condemned Congress for denying ex-CSA states representation. *Unconstitutional!* Most in Congress were unfazed as they went about tending to the nation's business.

On Monday, December 18, 1865, early business in the House included the filing of a number of citizens' requests, which would be referred to the appropriate committee—the Committee on Naval Affairs, the Committee on Commerce, the Committee on the Post Office and Post Roads, for example. Representative Henry Raymond from New York presented a petition from naval officers asking for a pay raise. Buckeye State representative William Lawrence submitted one from his constituents asking for a mail route from New Carlisle to Dayton.

As usual, the representatives put forth resolutions. Samuel Moulton (Republican–Illinois) resolved that President Johnson should "communicate to this House" why Jeff Davis, "this great criminal," had not yet been tried for treason. Others reported on bills awaiting the president's approval (his signature) or disapproval (his written veto). One was H.R. 23: "An act to prevent the spread of foreign diseases among the cattle of the United States."

The most dramatic happening in the House that day was Thad Stevens's speech on Reconstruction. "It matters but little," he said, whether you considered the CSA states "conquered territories" (as he and other radicals did) or saw them as being in suspended animation (as the president did). Bottom line: they were not alive to the nation. "Dead men cannot raise themselves. Dead States cannot restore their existence." If they can't, "in whom does the Constitution place the power?" he asked rhetorically. "Not in the judicial branch of Government, for it only adjudicates and does not prescribe laws. Not in the Executive, for he only executes and cannot make laws." Stevens reminded

Connecticut-born Gideon Welles, secretary of the navy. He quit the Democratic Party in the mid-1850s because of its support of slavery, then returned to the party after the war because he felt that suffrage should be left to the states. During the Civil War, Welles turned the piddling Union Navy into a force that was second only to Great Britain's navy. Highlights include adding ironclad ships to the fleet and orchestrating the successful blockade of Southern ports. The Union Navy, which had never banned blacks and which was not segregated, started recruiting blacks early on in the war and about eighteen thousand served (about 15 percent of the force).

Thaddeus Stevens, a graduate of Dartmouth College and onetime teacher. As a youngster in Vermont, Stevens was the butt of jokes and taunts because of his clubfoot and attendant limp. His mother (a domestic servant) worked herself to the bone so he could get an education (his father had abandoned the family). Stevens became a lawyer and eventually settled in Lancaster, Pennsylvania. In the 1830s, he successfully fought for Pennsylvania not to abolish a law that created free public schools. He lost the battle for black men to retain their right to vote in the state (taken away in a rewrite of its constitution in the late 1830s). Stevens was first elected to the U.S. House of Representatives in 1848. He wore a wig because an extreme case of alopecia early in life left him totally bald.

his colleagues (who needed no reminding) that the Constitution gave Congress the authority to admit states into the Union. "Congress—the Senate and the House of Representatives, with the concurrence of the President—is the only power that can act in the matter."

But before Congress even considered readmitting rebel states, it needed to change the way states were allotted representatives, Stevens insisted, "from Federal numbers to actual voters." A state's number of representatives has always been based on population, according to the latest federal census, which the Constitution mandated for this purpose. The larger a state's population, the more representatives it has, and thus the louder its voice.

To keep the more populous slaveholding states from being deafening, the framers of the Constitution based a state's representation on the total number of free people and three-fifths of its enslaved people. For example, in 1860, South Carolina's population was about 703,000: 88 "Indians"; 9,914 free blacks; 291,300 whites; and 402,406 enslaved people (with no data in the categories "Half-Breeds" and "Asiatics"). After the war, with slavery abolished, and assuming no major change in population, blacks who had been enslaved in South Carolina would be counted not as three-fifths (about 240,000) but as the more than 400,000 whole people they were. As a result, South Carolina would be entitled to more representatives—but the majority race in the state would have no voice because only white men could vote.

Stevens thought it obscene for former slave states to get increased congressional representation if black men were denied the vote. He also feared that if nothing changed, the solidly Democratic South combined with Democratic strongholds in the North would add up to disaster for the Republican Party. Democrats "will at the very first election take possession of the White House and the halls of Congress. I need not depict the ruin that would follow." But he did. Among other things, Stevens foresaw the "reestablishment of slavery."

Congress's authority to admit states and the basis of congressional representation weren't the only issues on Stevens's mind. He urged Congress to do more for recently freed people. "If we do not furnish them with homesteads, and hedge them around with protective laws; if we leave them to the legislation of their late masters, we had better have left them in bondage." If Congress did nothing—"if we fail in this great duty now, when we have the power"—then it deserved to be damned by "all future ages," he said.

Stevens also called upon his colleagues to condemn the doctrine of white supremacy. He pointed out that South Carolina's governor, Benjamin Perry, "and other provisional governors and orators proclaim that 'this is the white man's Government.' The whole copperhead party, pandering to the lowest prejudices of the ignorant, repeat the cuckoo cry, 'This is the white man's Government.'" In a jab at the president, no doubt, he added, "Demagogues of all parties, even some high in authority, gravely shout, 'This is the white man's Government.'" To Stevens, this was madness. "What is implied by this? That one race of men are to have the exclusive right forever to rule this nation . . . while all other races . . . are to be their subjects, and have no voice in making the laws and choosing the rulers by whom they are to be governed. Wherein does this differ from slavery except in degree?"

That same day, Secretary of State Seward certified that the Thirteenth Amendment to the Constitution had been adopted. Since Lincoln's death, six more states had ratified it (Connecticut, New Hampshire, South Carolina, Alabama, North Carolina, and Georgia). Congress had the necessary approval of three-fourths of the states. America had officially abolished slavery!

In spring 1787, several years after the American Revolution, George Washington, Benjamin Franklin, James Madison, Alexander Hamilton, Roger Sherman (ancestor of General Sherman), and fifty other delegates from all but one of the thirteen states (Rhode Island) convened in Philadelphia to revise the nation's first constitution, the Articles of Confederation (1777). These men, several of whom, like Washington, were slaveholders, set about creating "a more perfect union" in their interests. Working in what became Independence Hall, they hammered out how the nation would work: from the rights and responsibilities of the executive, legislative, and judicial branches, and the balance of power between the federal government and the states, to how the Constitution could be amended, codifying slavery in the process. The final document consisted of the preamble ("We the People . . .") and seven articles. It became the supreme law of the land on June 21, 1788, after nine states ratified it.

Just as that news sparked both mourning and jubilation around the nation, so Thad Stevens's speech triggered diverse—and intense—discussions in the capital and beyond. "The ensuing debate in the House and Senate flamed over all creation," wrote W.E.B. Du Bois. "Congressional amendments of every sort poured into Congress concerning the national and Confederate debt, the civil rights of freedmen . . . the basis of representation, payment for slaves and the future powers of Federal government and the states. Argument swirled in a maelstrom of logic." In this vortex, two questions loomed large for Du Bois. One: "Shall the South be rewarded for unsuccessful secession by increased political power?" Two: "Can the freed Negro be a part of American democracy?"

"CROSSING THE PLAINS BEFORE THE PACIFIC RAILROAD WAS BUILT," from **The Great Industries of the United States** (1872), co-authored by Horace Greeley. Before rail service to the West Coast, crossing the Great Plains could take up to six months and cost more than a thousand dollars. The waterway route was also costly and time-consuming (about three months). One route entailed catching a ship from an East Coast or Gulf of Mexico port that headed down and around the tip of South America, then up to the West Coast. Wagon trains heading west increased because of the 1862 Homestead Act. Intended to encourage white western migration, it allowed heads of households to acquire 160 acres for a nominal fee.

The press kept the public up to speed on the shake-up Republicans were causing, along with other news, like the popularity of a short story about a jumping frog by Mark Twain, recently a struggling freelance journalist, soon a literary star. Progress of the Pacific Railroad was also in the news.

The viability of the steam locomotive had sparked a revolution in travel. By 1860, railway mileage had gone from piddling to over thirty thousand miles of track, most of it in the East. With the discovery of gold in California (late 1840s) and gold and silver in Nevada (late 1850s), westward-ho types—merchants,

When a gang robbed a bank in Liberty, Missouri, of about sixty thousand dollars on February 13, 1866, they pulled off a first, many believe: a bank heist in broad daylight. Eighteen-year-old Jesse James was one of the masterminds and already a bandit. During the war, he rode with a band of guerrilla warriors for the Confederacy. Their crimes included bushwhacking Union soldiers and robbing trains.

manufacturers, and railroad company chiefs—lobbied the federal government to make railroads a national priority. An iron-horse passage to the West Coast was vital, they argued. In 1861, Omaha, Nebraska, was the farthest west trains went.

During the Civil War, Congress passed the first railroad act, creating a roughly two-thousand-mile line to the Far West. The legislation permitted the Union Pacific Railroad Company to build this railroad east from Sacramento, California; the Central Pacific Railroad Company, west from Omaha. The government would give the companies millions of dollars in loans and subsidies and millions of acres of land—land they could later sell or mine for gold, coal, and other natural resources. Much of the land was home to Shoshone, Sioux, and other peoples the ignorant called "Injuns." So while Johnny Rebs and Billy Yanks were battling it out, mostly in the South, the Union had also been waging a campaign in the West to clear the railroad's path of "Injuns"—sometimes by treaty, sometimes by gun.

When the Pacific Railroad was just a dream and William Tecumseh Sherman just a captain, he had written to a future U.S. senator, his younger brother John, of Central Pacific's daunting task of getting track through the Sierra Nevada Mountains: "If it is ever built," said Cump of the Pacific Railroad, "it will be the work of giants." Giants were in short supply. It was mostly poor immigrants who built the Pacific Railroad. Early on, only a handful of the workers were Chinese. Most had come to America after the California Gold Rush kicked off. Then, in early 1865, in search of more cheap labor, the Central Pacific Railroad Company recruited men from famine-ravaged parts of China to chisel/pick/shovel/blast tunnels through the Sierra Nevada Mountains and do other work for lower wages than those paid to men from Ireland, Germany, Wales, and other European countries. Several thousand Chinese men were working on the railroad by January 1866. Many Americans felt that's all they should do—then leave.

In early February 1866, a few days before the legendary bank robbery in Liberty, Missouri, an article headlined "Interview of the Colored Committee with the President" appeared in Rhode Island's *Providence Evening Press*, along with a multitude of ads—pianofortes; Dr. Ruoff's "American Hair Renewer!"; the mail-order services of astrologer Madame Perregault; and "BONES WANTED" (by a chemical company). The Providence newspaper was one of many that covered this historic meeting at the Executive Mansion.

The black delegation met with President Johnson on February 7, 1866. Its members included Pennsylvania lumber merchant and former Underground Railroad worker William Whipper. Fred Douglass was also there. So was his oldest son, Lewis. Along with his brother Charles, Lewis had fought for the Union, with the 54th Massachusetts, the first black regiment raised in the North, for which their father had been a recruiter.

*Maryland-born Frederick Douglass, who escaped slavery in 1838, when he was about twenty years old. Douglass was one of about forty men at the historic women's rights convention in Seneca Falls in 1848, where Elizabeth Cady Stanton read the **Woman's Declaration of Rights and Sentiments**. He wholeheartedly endorsed her call for women's suffrage. "Slavery is not abolished until the black man has the ballot," Douglass said about a month after Lee's surrender. The occasion was the American Anti-Slavery Society's convention at New York City's Church of the Puritan. Members were to decide whether to dissolve the organization in light of the imminent passage of the Thirteenth Amendment. The vote was 118 to 48 in favor of remaining alive and kicking as a civil rights organization: to continue to "teach the nation justice," as member Anna Dickinson said.*

The first to address the president was former Rhode Island hotelier and caterer George Downing, who ran the U.S. House of Representatives dining room. "We are not satisfied with an amendment prohibiting slavery but we wish that amendment enforced with appropriate legislation," he told Johnson. Downing also pressed for suffrage. "We are Americans—native-born Americans—We are citizens . . . we cherish the hope that we may be fully enfranchised, not only here in this district, but throughout the land." Blacks in D.C. had recently petitioned Congress for the right to vote.

Fred Douglass asserted that if blacks were good enough to pay taxes, shed blood in battles, and obey the laws, they were good enough to have privileges of citizenship, just like white folks. President Johnson responded with the line that he was willing to be black people's Moses. He advised patience, and added that it might be best for blacks to leave America.

After the delegation left, the president raged to his private secretary. He cursed the black men. Of Douglass, he said, "I know" him, "he's just like any nigger." But the president didn't know Douglass or anyone else in the delegation. Men like Douglass and Downing, blacks who achieved and excelled, blasted the myth of black inferiority that people like Johnson clung to largely to prop up their bogus claim of white superiority.

The issue of the *Providence Evening Press* that reported on the Douglass-Downing delegation also had an alert about immigrants: "Colonies of Europeans are coming into Texas. The Poles are settling on Trinity River, near Palestine. The Germans and others from the Northwestern States are settling in colonies." As well, the newspaper had an item on the recent New Hampshire Democratic Convention. The conventioneers pledged support for President Johnson's efforts to "secure to all the States immediate representation in Congress, and their full right under the Constitution as States of the Union." They vowed to "stand by him as long as he stands by the Constitution." Standing up for ex-CSA states was precisely what Andy Johnson planned to do.

On February 9, 1866, Congress sent him a bill that would make the Freedmen's Bureau permanent and expand its mission. The bill's provisions included giving freed people and war-wrecked loyal whites a chance to rent no more than forty acres of public domain land for a nominal fee with an option to buy. It also called for the federal government to build schools, hospitals, and other institutions for blacks.

President Johnson saw this bill as unfair to white people. Congress, he said, had "never founded schools for any class of our own people, not even for the orphans of those who have fallen in the defense of the Union," and had "never deemed itself authorized to expend the public money for the rent or purchase of homes for the thousands, not to say millions, of the white race, who are honestly toiling from day to day for their subsistence."

Never mind that millions of blacks were destitute. Never mind that they lived under laws and customs designed to keep them that way. Never mind that along with individual slaveholders and businesses in both the North and the South, the federal government had profited from slave labor—most symbolically in the construction of the Capitol Building and the Executive Mansion Andy Johnson occupied. Never mind that the bill proposed to help needy white people, too. *Veto!*

The president chided Congress for devising such a bill when most of the states in the South, where it would have the greatest impact, had no representation in Congress. After all, the Freedmen's Bureau initiatives would be at taxpayers' expense. "The principle is firmly fixed in the minds of the American people that there should be no taxation without representation," Johnson stated, referencing a battle cry of the American Revolution.

The Republicans had the necessary two-thirds majority to pass the bill, despite the president's veto, but not the unity. Some of them were reluctant to buck Johnson lest they ruin the possibility of Congress and the president working together on Reconstruction. The reluctant became the resistant and because they did, there weren't enough votes to override Johnson's veto.

About a month later, in March 1866, Congress sent the president a bill intended to defang the black codes: "An act to protect all persons in the United States in their civil rights, and furnish the means of their vindication." The bill declared anyone born in America—"excluding Indians not taxed"—a U.S. citizen. "Indians not taxed"—and not included in the federal census—were Native Americans who were *in* America but not *of* it: those living within their independent nations and on reservations. "Indians taxed" were the minority of Native Americans who had assimilated. One example is General Grant's staffer Lieutenant Colonel Ely Parker, the Senecan who had written out the surrender terms at Appomattox.

The civil rights bill stated that all citizens (except convicted criminals) were entitled to the same rights—from making contracts and suing to buying and selling real estate (but not the right to vote). Another right: federal government protection of their rights. *Veto!* President Johnson found the idea of black citizenship vomitous. Equally nauseating for him, "the Chinese of the Pacific States, Indians subject to taxation, [and] the people called Gypsies" would also be citizens. What's more, the bill trampled states' rights, he argued. Was a citizen of the nation necessarily a citizen of a state? he asked. Wasn't that a matter for each state to decide?

This time the Republicans had the unity. The Freedmen's Bureau and civil rights bills had been drafted and talked about around the same time. Johnson had given some people the impression that he would not veto the civil rights bill. That's why some Republicans had voted not to override his veto on the first bill. They had been duped.

In early April 1866, Congress overrode the president's veto for the making of what is known as the Civil Rights Act of 1866, the first broad piece of legislation passed over a presidential veto. Congress had flexed its muscles like never before. Then, in late April, the Joint Committee on Reconstruction proposed a fourteenth amendment to the Constitution. This amendment said that U.S. citizens, whether by birth or naturalization, were also citizens of their states. It also contained a carrot and stick for the cause of black male suffrage: a state's representation in Congress was to be based on its population

"SCENES IN MEMPHIS, TENNESSEE, DURING THE RIOTS—BURNING A FREEDMEN'S SCHOOL-HOUSE" *from the cover of the May 26, 1866, issue of* **Harper's Weekly**. *When a black-white altercation broke out on Memphis's South Street on May 1, 1866, "word was sent to police head-quarters, and the whole force at once proceeded to the scene of the fray, being joined on the way thither by armed and excited citizens," according to the* **New York Times**. *"Meanwhile the firing had brought other negroes to the spot, some armed with clubs and some with revolvers, so that by the time the police force came up the two parties were about equal in number." When white troops arrived on the scene, "the negroes were quickly dispersed and driven in every direction." That evening, whites, emboldened by the police, resumed the violence, keeping it up into the next day. When it was over, much of the black community lay in ruins. Republicans pointed to the Memphis riot as proof that the ex-CSA states were still too savage, too rebellious—not ready for reunion.*

of men, age twenty-one and older, who had the right to vote. This would have the greatest impact on the Southern states, with their large black populations. Andy Johnson denounced the amendment. Legions in the South howled in horror. Congress passed the Fourteenth Amendment in mid-June 1866. By then it contained a passage that put a check on men who had held public office before the war and then held office in the CSA: they were barred from holding state or national office until Congress said so.

Two states in the North were quick to ratify the amendment: Connecticut (June 25) and New Hampshire (July 6). In the South, only Tennessee (July 19). Congress made an example of Andy Johnson's Tennessee. On July 24, the Volunteer State became the first ex-CSA state readmitted to the Union.

Workers gather crops on an unidentified site of a Civil War battle in this engraving captioned "HARVEST ON HISTORIC FIELDS— A SCENE AT THE SOUTH" in the July 20, 1867, issue of **Harper's Weekly**. Sharecropping became the dominant labor system in the still very agrarian South. Landowners provided the land, housing (usually a shack), and just about everything needed to work the land (seed, animals, equipment). Workers (usually whole families) received a percentage of the harvest (anywhere from 25 percent to 50 percent) instead of wages. Workers bought necessities on credit at stores, often owned by the people for whom they worked. These stores usually charged high interest rates—in some cases over 50 percent. Many sharecroppers stayed poor and in debt.

To those who accused Republicans of riding roughshod over the ex-CSA states, people like Thad Stevens would say that they were just exercising due diligence.

Between December and June 1866, the Joint Committee on Reconstruction reviewed reports of Southern murders and "outrages." Along with newspapers, Freedmen's Bureau agents had noted and would continue to record such incidents.

The litany of persecution in Texas includes the actions of Jerome deBlanc, a Liberty County planter. In August 1865, he handcuffed a black man and his wife, "then brutally struck and kicked them" because their two sons "had left the plantation without permission." DeBlanc also "tied up and beat" another black man "because he refused to contract."

In October 1865, in Houston County, "on the road from Crockett to Huntsville," James Murphy shot Boston McDaniel dead. "Cause: The Freedman did not take off his hat to Murphy when he passed him."

Cause: The man said he was "too sick to pick cotton." That's why, on October 5, 1865, in Fort Bend County, H. Dimlavy beat Miles "severely with his heavy walking stick, cutting his head and shoulders."

Cause: "Lazy." So, in October 1865, in Harris County, William McMahon beat Adeline "brutally over the head and face with a paddle, marking her up badly."

Cause: "Did not do enough work." That's why, in December 1865, Dr. John Fisher of Walker County "drew a pistol on Herod Hudson . . . drove him from the field where he was at work, into the gin house, made a colored man beat him and place a rope around his neck." The doctor then "tied [Hudson's] hands behind him, blindfolded him and drew him up by the rope until he had partially choked him and then let him down. Then drove him off."

Texas did not have a monopoly on violence. In Murfreesboro, Tennessee, in June 1865, after Bee Whitney and his wife had worked Isaac Rucker's fields for one-third of the crop, Rucker "attempted to drive them off without pay." When the couple stood their ground, Rucker "beat Whitney's wife on the head and side, badly, with a piece of board—knocking her down, and this only six days before the birth of her child."

Freedmen's Bureau agents did not always provide complete information. Sometimes there was a blank in the place of a victim's or assailant's name. Sometimes they recorded no "cause," just the crime, leaving their superiors and the future to wonder why in April 1865, on a plantation near Gallatin, Tennessee, two white men, Thomas Perry and James Morton, snatched a black man, Gilbert McGee, from his plow, tied him to a tree, then "whipped, shot, and finally beheaded" him.

"Civil Authorities did nothing." So ended more than a few entries in a report on violence in Louisiana. There, in Amite City, on an early July 1865 evening, Marshal Amile Lovitt asked a black man en route from church for his pass. When the man replied that "he had none, nor did he consider it necessary now," the marshal "struck him over the head with his pistol, and on his running off fired at him twice, wounding a white man who was standing near. When the freedman reached the main street, a man in a coffee house emptied his revolver at him."

In a Louisiana hamlet a few miles from Opelousas, a desire to praise God was an offense in mid-June 1866. Captain J. S. Clark reported that, in a building they had rented for worship services, about a dozen blacks "were arrested for disturbing the peace before they had commenced their exercise" and each fined four dollars. Cause: Some worshippers had "previously preached or prayed too loud."

Politically and racially motivated violence was also rife in Southern states that had not seceded. In early August 1865, "on the public road at Port Republic," in Calvert County, Maryland, two white men, James and John Brown, struck another white man, McVeigh Beverly, with their guns and shot at him. Cause: He had "voted for Abraham Lincoln." Several days before, John Bond, Jr., a CSA Army veteran, had beaten Beverly with a club. That summer, elsewhere in Maryland, eleven white men had beaten a black man, Isaac Craig, "till life was nearly extinct and attempted to hang him but desisted." Cause: Craig had "cheered a speaker who alluded to the Emancipation Proclamation" at a political meeting. One of his assailants was a judge. Shortly before they attacked Craig, four of the men "badly beat" a recently discharged white soldier, Marshall Wilkeson. Cause: Wilkeson had "declared himself a Union man."

"I have the honor to make the following report of the state of affairs in this district for ten days ending May 20, 1866," began a letter to a Freedmen's Bureau commissioner in Hamburg, South Carolina, from a junior officer, Captain C. R. Beeby, stationed in Abbeville. "On Saturday night, May 12, about ten o'clock a freedman by the name of Elbert MacAdams was taken from his house by an unknown man and shot three times and then had his throat cut and was dragged into the woods about a hundred yards from his house, where he was found dead on Sunday morning."

All Captain Beeby knew was that "the freedman had come to see his wife who lived on Basil Callaham's plantation, about 16 miles from here." Beeby had Callaham and two other men arrested but "after an examination released them as we could prove nothing against them and as yet I have obtained no clue to the parties who done the deed or any reason why it was done." Captain Beeby added, "Freedmen report to the office every day that they are being driven off." Beeby apparently had little free time. Cause: "My

Massachusetts-born Rufus Saxton. In 1862, in Port Royal, South Carolina, he raised the First South Carolina Volunteers, renamed the 33rd United States Colored Troops when it became the Union Army's official first black regiment. After the war, Saxton was the Freedmen's Bureau's assistant commissioner for South Carolina, Georgia, and Florida. In January 1866, President Johnson removed him because Saxton was allied with the radicals.

Member of the Joint Committee on Reconstruction George Sewall Boutwell, former governor of Massachusetts and commissioner of the Bureau of Internal Revenue (today's Internal Revenue Service). Boutwell entered the U.S. House of Representatives in 1863. He and Thad Stevens were two of the Radical Republicans on the committee. The others were Representative Elihu Washburne (Illinois) and Senators Jacob Howard (Michigan) and George Williams (Oregon). The seven moderates included Representative John Bingham (Ohio) and committee chair Senator William Fessenden (Maine). One of the three Democrats was Senator Reverdy Johnson (Maryland), who had briefly served as counsel for alleged Booth co-conspirator Mary Surratt.

time is entirely taken up looking into the reasons and seeing that they get their rights."

The Joint Committee on Reconstruction also interviewed dozens of citizens, soldiers, and government officials. Nurse Clara Barton testified about her encounters in Georgia. She had gone there after getting ahold of the death records from the CSA prisoner-of-war camp near Andersonville, then petitioning Secretary of War Stanton for permission to take a team down there to find and mark Union soldiers' graves. While in Georgia, Barton met some poor souls, illiterate and ignorant of the law, who had been told that because Abe Lincoln was dead, they were no longer free. They rightly suspected trickery, but had concluded that Lincoln was really alive and therefore they were really free. Barton clarified that the two matters had nothing to do with each other. Yes, Lincoln was dead. Yes, "they were free as I was."

"What is [the freedmen's] disposition in regard to purchasing land, and what is the disposition of the landowners in reference to selling land to Negroes?" the committee asked General Rufus Saxton.

"The object which the freedman has most at heart is the purchase of land," he replied. "They all desire to get small homesteads." He felt there was "scarcely any

Clara Barton, daughter of the Bay State. She had braved horrors of war numerous times to transport food, medicine, and other supplies to Union soldiers and to nurse them in field hospitals. The "Angel of the Battlefield" co-founded the American Red Cross in the early 1880s.

sacrifice too great for them to make to accomplish this," but that whites "desire to keep the Negroes landless, and as nearly in a condition of slavery as it is possible for them to do."

"WHY NOT HANG THAD STEVENS!"

This engraving was captioned "SECRET MEETING OF SOUTHERN UNIONISTS" when it appeared in the August 4, 1866, issue of **Harper's Weekly**. Artist-journalist Alfred Waud had spent time with a group like this in a small town in Louisiana where Republicans were few in number. "Employment is kept from them, and covert insult—sometimes more—is heaped upon them," reported Waud. The lookout was in place in case their political foes decided to "repeat the little trick" of shooting into the house, then "running away in the dark."

Ex-Confederates had their defenders. When General John Tarbell testified before the Joint Committee on Reconstruction, he spoke well of them. Tarbell, a Republican, had purchased a plantation in Scott County, Mississippi.

"Do you apprehend any difficulty in the management of your plantation, growing out of the fact that you are a Northern man?" Representative George

Boutwell asked Tarbell. No, the general replied. When asked about ex-Confederates' loyalty to the Union, he said that they had rebelled "fully in the belief of the right of secession" and had "staked their fortunes and their lives on that issue," but after losing the war had "utterly and forever abandoned the idea." Tarbell acknowledged that some Southerners were highly critical of "what are called the radicals of the North." He didn't see that as a sign of disloyalty, just "a difference of political opinion."

Tarbell's low opinion of blacks probably had something to do with why he got along with whites in the South. He didn't think blacks had much "capacity for future improvement." People like Tarbell didn't carry much weight with the committee, which issued its final report in late June 1866. The report said that the ten Southern states did not deserve representation in Congress. In mid-July, over Johnson's veto, Congress passed a revised Freedmen's Bureau bill. (Gone was the land grant provision, and the agency would remain temporary.) That same month, an incident in Louisiana convinced more Northerners that Congress was right to override the president and right not to go light on the rebels.

On July 30, 1866, in New Orleans, Republicans held a convention to

TRAITORS TO THEIR RACE.

Admitting that the Abolitionists, however mistaken in the means, really do wish to benefit the negroes of the South, it is then a matter of doubt for which they work hardest—the good of the negroes or the evil of the white people. It is atrocious, and indeed amazing beyond conception, how any man or woman in the North dares to meddle at all with whites and negroes in the South, or how a citizen of Massachusetts dares to go into Virginia and dictate to a citizen of that State his relation to his negro. If they have any legal right growing out of the government or Union created by Washington, Jefferson, &c., to do this, or to "abolish slavery," as they call it, then the names of Washington and Jefferson should be execrated in all coming time as those of the vilest traitors and villains that ever betrayed a people. But they have not—Washington, and Jefferson, and Lee, and others who brought about the Union with Massachusetts, &c., would have suffered martyrdom and would rather have died at the stake than thus betray their descendants, or rather than give the men of Massachusetts any legal right to "abolish slavery." But it is, nevertheless, the fact—citizens of Massachusetts do go into Virginia and do dictate to them such relations to their negroes as suit the ideas or theories of the former, and we repeat, it is a matter of doubt in which they are most earnest—a morbid and devilish desire to benefit the negroes, or to injure the white people. The devilish and unsexed women, who go down to teach the negroes, exhibit the same phase of devilishness; they teach Sambo his alphabet at the same moment that they teach him to insult his former mistress, and with the Lord's Prayer they teach the poor wretch to hate his master. Indeed, by an inexorable necessity that links evil to evil forever, this mutual or coequal devilment pervades all Abolitiondom. During the war, the Abolition generals were just as fierce to steal cotton as they were to destroy the sources of cotton production, and every day, in the vile concern they call a Congress, they strive, through tariffs and all kinds of plunder schemes, to rob the white people just in proportion as they profess to benefit the negro. Perhaps this is a law, an inexorable necessity, that their father, the devil, imposes on them—they must hate the whites just to the extent that they love the negroes, or in other words, must be traitors and enemies of their own race in exact proportion as they give themselves up to the nasty and obscene love of a lower race.

*Blacks are declared "a lower race," Congress "vile," and white women who went south to teach blacks "devilish" and "unsexed" in this item from the July 7, 1866, issue of **The New York Day-Book**. It boasted "the LARGEST CIRCULATION of any weekly Democratic paper published in the North."*

About two hundred blacks turned out to support Republicans in New Orleans who wanted to redraft Louisiana's constitution. They, along with the convention delegates, met with violence inside and outside the hall where the event was held. By the time troops arrived on the scene, more than thirty blacks and three whites (all Republicans) were dead and more than a hundred people were injured. In this engraving, which appeared in the September 8, 1866, issue of **Harper's Weekly**, *legendary illustrator Thomas Nast captures how the New Orleans riot sent chills up the spines of Union men elsewhere in the South.*

toss the state constitution created under Lincoln's Ten Percent Plan and draft a new one that granted black men the right to vote and took it away from certain ex-Confederates. Angry whites reacted with what General Phil Sheridan called "an absolute massacre."

The New Orleans riot was not a random act of violence; it was planned, which was becoming the norm. White resistance to black empowerment was "organized intimidation and terrorism," recalled Democrat Samuel Cox (a representative from Ohio, and later New York). "It was directed against the colored people and against their white allies." White allies born in the South were scorned as "scalawags," a term originally applied to worthless livestock. Those from the North, "carpetbaggers," after a cheap variety of luggage made from old carpets. Many Northerners carried such bags in their journeys south. Most were on government business or a humanitarian mission, and some were opportunists eager to take advantage of Southern chaos and misery, buying up foreclosed property and entering politics to enrich themselves.

The groups that persecuted blacks, scalawags, and carpetbaggers included "The Brotherhood" and "The Pale Faces." Many of them folded into the group formed in Pulaski, Tennessee, as a social club for CSA Army veterans. It eventually took the name Ku Klux Klan (KKK). Sheriffs, shopkeepers, blacksmiths, judges, barkeeps, bankers, stable hands, and mayors joined the KKK. Andy Johnson's old nemesis Nathan Bedford Forrest would become its first Grand Wizard. His minions would maim and murder thousands of people who disagreed with the notion that America was the white man's country.

As for the highest-ranking proponent of that ideology, President Johnson embarked on a speaking tour in late August 1866. Many congressional seats would be up in the fall. He aimed to get out the vote for Democrats. In his "swing around the circle" tour, Johnson traveled around the Northeast and Midwest before returning to Washington, D.C., in mid-September. In his set speech, he spoke about the loyalty of whites in ex-CSA states, the need to hurry up and restore their representation in Congress, the sanctity of states' rights, and the evil of the Fourteenth Amendment.

Johnson's tour was a wreck. Back then, it was tacky for the president to engage in overtly political campaign speeches. Worse, Johnson often veered off into attacks on Congress. When he addressed a crowd in Cleveland, Ohio, he cast Thad Stevens and other radicals as satanic, claiming that they "once talked about forming a 'league with hell and a covenant with the devil.'" The president boasted that even with the "power of hell, death and Stevens with all his powers combined, there is no power that can control me, save you the people and the God that spoke me into existence." He characterized Congress as useless and counterproductive. "Has it done anything to restore the Union of the States? But, on the contrary, has it not done everything to prevent it?"

Along with cheers—"Bully!" "Hurrah for Andy!"—Johnson got plenty of jeers. "Shut up!" a crowd shouted in Indianapolis. When it came to handling hecklers, the president often stooped to their level. During one speech, to the shout "Hang Jeff Davis!" Johnson shot back, "Why not hang Thad Stevens and Wendell Phillips!" (Phillips, a dynamic orator, was president of the postwar American Anti-Slavery Society.)

There were rumors of presidential drunkenness during the tour, but whiskey was not to blame for Andy Johnson's tirades. It was his racism and his

KKK leader Nathan Bedford Forrest had risen to general in the CSA Army, with a particular hatred for black regiments. He once offered a thousand dollars for the head of any commander of one. Northerners held him responsible for the Fort Pillow massacre (1864): about fifteen hundred cavalrymen under his command took the Union-held Tennessee fort. Almost half of the Union's six hundred black and white troops, along with many women and children, were killed. Northerners claimed most were murdered as they surrendered.

rage at the Radical Republicans. Even some of his supporters were appalled by Johnson's outbursts. "Depend upon it, this sort of thing cannot go on without hurting us more than it helps," wrote one Democrat to another.

Republicans had many victories in the congressional elections. Looking into the new year, the radicals were dead set on overthrowing Presidential Reconstruction and instituting a *congressional* plan.

"MAKING A WHIPPING-POST OF THE SOUTH"

*From the March 20, 1869, issue of **Harper's Weekly**: Washington, D.C.'s Howard University under construction. The school was Congress's response to a group of whites' desire to start a school aimed at educating people who would serve black communities. The school was named after one of its founders (and an early president), General Howard, head of the Freedmen's Bureau. Howard University was one of many HBCUs (historically black colleges and universities) founded during Reconstruction. Among the others are Fisk University (Nashville, Tennessee), Morehouse College (Atlanta, Georgia), and Talladega College (Talladega, Alabama). Though created for blacks, these schools did not deny anyone admission because of race or ethnicity. Like Howard, some were created through acts of legislation (state and federal); others, by black and white philanthropists and churches.*

"We are making a nation," Thad Stevens would one day stress in a House debate on Reconstruction. And while Congress grappled with America's political landscape, it also attended to the nation's infrastructure. Between January and March 1867 alone, Congress passed a bevy of bills to that end. Examples include expenditures and caretaking directives for dozens of

national cemeteries, such as enclosing them "with good and substantial stone or iron fence." Over $4 million was slated for harbor work and other improvements on waterways, in places as different as Sheboygan, Wisconsin, and Boston, Massachusetts.

During the same period, Republicans pushed through—almost always over the president's veto—some radical legislation to advance their cause: control of Reconstruction.

January 8—"An act to regulate the elective franchise in the District of Columbia": All men, age twenty-one and older, born or naturalized in the United States and living in D.C. for at least a year could vote there. Exceptions included "paupers," convicted felons, and men who had "given aid and comfort to the rebels."

January 21—"An act to repeal section thirteen of 'An act to suppress insurrection, to punish treason and rebellion, to seize and confiscate the property of rebels, and for other purposes,' approved July seventeenth, eighteen hundred and sixty-two." This act with a long title had a quick point: it stripped Johnson of the power to pardon any more ex-Confederates. (Many acts had titles that seem absurdly long to the average person, which is why they became known as something much shorter.)

January 25—An act that said men could not be denied the vote in existing and future territories "on account of race, color, or previous condition of servitude."

March 2—"An act to incorporate the Howard University in the District of Columbia."

March 2—An act known as the Tenure of Office Act: the president could not fire certain civil servants without Senate approval. The act covered cabinet officers, who were to keep their jobs "during the term of the President by whom they may have been appointed and for one month thereafter." Concern that Johnson would fire Secretary of War Stanton had prompted this provision.

Also during early 1867, Congress issued its master plan for Reconstruction: "An act for the more efficient government of the rebel states." With the exception of Tennessee, which had swiftly approved the Fourteenth Amendment and been readmitted to the Union, the ex-CSA states were demoted to conquered land and put under martial law. They became five military districts: Virginia, the first; North Carolina and South Carolina, the second; Georgia, Alabama, and Florida, the third; Mississippi and Arkansas, the fourth; and Louisiana and Texas, the fifth.

District commanders were duty-bound "to protect all persons in their rights of person and property, to suppress insurrection, disorder, and violence, and to punish, or cause to be punished, all disturbers of the public peace and criminals." If district commanders felt it necessary, they could have lawbreakers tried by a military tribunal. Another duty was to supervise the election of delegates to state conventions for creating new constitutions. These constitutions had to be ratified by a majority of a state's registered voters.

Above all, these new state constitutions had to give black men the vote. That was crucial if blacks were to have a say in the remaking of their states and if the Republican Party was to have sway in the South. White Republicans (Southern-born and Northern transplants) were a definite minority there. But blacks were either a sizeable portion or a majority in the ex-CSA states (close to 60 percent in South Carolina, more than 50 percent in Louisiana and Mississippi). Because the Republican Party was the party of emancipation and their best hope for true liberty, black men would vote Republican, with rare exception. And vote they could, for delegates to the congressionally mandated state constitutional conventions. When Congress approved a state's constitution and a state ratified the Fourteenth Amendment—back in the Union.

President Johnson was livid. He didn't care that blacks in the CSA states were catching hell. He didn't care that some white Southerners would go to war again if they thought they could win. As he saw it, whites were being victimized,

*From the April 6, 1867, issue of **Harper's Weekly**: district commanders of the states placed under martial law. Ex-rebels in Louisiana and Texas had reason to tremble when they heard who was commander of their district: Philip Henry Sheridan (right panel, with handlebar mustache). Sheridan had commanded "The Burning": the 1864 torching of homes, farmland, factories, and other infrastructure in Virginia's Shenandoah Valley, the Confederacy's key source of food and other supplies. Between Sheridan and flag, Edward Otho Cresap (commandant of Arkansas and Mississippi). At left of right panel, the bearded John McAllister Schofield (Virginia). At left of left panel, Daniel Edgar Sickles (the Carolinas); in background of left panel, with beard, John Pope (Georgia, Alabama, and Florida). Center, Ulysses S. Grant (still general-in-chief of the army); to his right is George Henry Thomas, commander of the Pacific Division.*

stomped on "to protect niggers," he told a journalist. In his veto, Johnson said the Reconstruction bill was in gross "conflict with the plainest provisions of the Constitution." If South Carolina and company were no longer valid states but conquered territories, how could they ratify an amendment? According to the Constitution, wasn't that a right reserved for states? Johnson also condemned Congress for strong-arming the ten ex-CSA states to let black men vote. "The negroes have not asked for the privilege of voting—the vast majority of them have no idea what it means," he lied. On March 2, 1867, Congress overrode the president's veto. What became known as the First Reconstruction Act marks the start of "Congressional Reconstruction."

Before March was out—and again over Johnson's veto—came the Second Reconstruction Act. It put district commanders in charge of elections for municipal and state offices, starting with voter registration. The process included an oath or affirmation that one was not an ex-felon and had played no part in the rebellion.

The fifth district's commander, General Sheridan, kicked scores of men from office, especially in Louisiana. When Johnson upbraided Sheridan, Congress fired back with the Third Reconstruction Act in mid-July 1867. It declared that district commanders could do what Sheridan had done. And if registrars thought someone taking the oath was lying—begone!

Months before the Third Reconstruction Act, the adamant Thad Stevens had proposed a bill to right some more wrongs. "The punishment of traitors has been wholly ignored by a treacherous Executive and by a sluggish Congress," he charged when he lobbied for his bill's passage in mid-March. Among other things, this bill, H.R. 29, called for all public land in the military districts to become the property of the federal government and land confiscated from rebels to remain confiscated. In certain cases, if land had been returned to any of them—seize it again. Some of the land was to be sold, with proceeds slated for Union soldiers' pension funds and ever-loyal whites in the South who had suffered property loss and damage at rebel hands. Much of the confiscated land was to be set aside for recently freed people living in a former CSA state since March 1861. Heads of households were to receive forty acres.

H.R. 29 never passed. There were not enough Republicans who believed, as Stevens did, that land reform was in order, that people who had been robbed of their liberty and labor were due reparations.

Even though the bill didn't pass, Stevens became all the more despised in the South. To propose such a bill was insult added to the grave injury of martial law. One man who captured what many Southerners felt was ex-CSA general Richard Taylor, whose deceased sister had been Jeff Davis's first wife and whose father, Zachary, had been the nation's twelfth president. In his memoirs, Richard Taylor looked back on Congressional Reconstruction as a time when Congress was "making a whipping-post of the South."

Taylor's compatriots sought solace in the "Lost Cause" movement, its name inspired by the 1866 book *The Lost Cause: A New Southern History of the War of the Confederates*. In Lost Cause thought, the CSA had waged a righteous war for states' rights. Its leaders—most notably Jeff Davis—were elevated to virtual sainthood. Lost Causers saw the South as a holy nation chosen by God to sustain what they believed was the sacred social order: white rule.

It was in spring 1867, at a clandestine convention in Nashville, Tennessee, that the KKK proclaimed itself the Invisible Empire of the South. Cause: Congressional Reconstruction.

"We are here tonight to tell the world, that after being enfranchised we are wise enough to know our rights and we are going to claim . . . every right that belongs to an American citizen," said Lawrence Berry at a Republican rally in spring 1867, probably a lot bigger than the one pictured here. Lawrence Berry was a Union League organizer working in Mobile, Alabama. The Union League was one of the Republican political clubs devoted to voter education and registration drives. This scene was captioned "ELECTIONEERING AT THE SOUTH" in the July 25, 1868, issue of Harper's Weekly.

On the wings of Congressional Reconstruction, blacks in the military districts seized the day. There were crash courses on the Constitution and the workings of the government in churches, homes, schools, and the cool of piney woods. Cookouts served up lectures on the power of the vote.

Congressional Reconstruction motivated more Northerners to lend their might to the grassroots organizing going on in the South—people like Reverend James Lynch, editor of the African Methodist Episcopal (AME) Church's newspaper, the *Christian Recorder*, headquartered in Philadelphia. Lynch resigned his post and went south, prompted by "convictions of duty to my race as deep as my own soul." His stomping ground was Mississippi; he became its secretary of state in 1869.

In the congressionally mandated constitutional conventions (1867–1869), more than 25 percent of the roughly one thousand delegates were black men. Some were farmworkers, blacksmiths, carpenters. Others were proprietors of prosperous enterprises (saloons, restaurants, grocery stores). Delegates included Major Johnson of Florida, an AME Church elder; Samuel Kelso of Virginia, a teacher; and Mobile, Alabama–born Moses Avery, son of a wealthy white man and an enslaved woman. Avery had served in the Union Navy and, after the war, as an editor of the *New Orleans Tribune*. During Congressional Reconstruction, more than two thousand black men held office by appointment or election. Some were postmasters, coroners, school superintendents, county treasurers, and judges. State senators: a little over a hundred. State representatives: almost seven hundred. Sixteen served in the U.S. Congress.

The **New Orleans Tribune**, *founded in 1864, was America's first black-interest daily newspaper. Because Louisiana had a large French-speaking population, there was usually a French and an English edition. Sometimes a single issue carried some news in French and some in English. From late 1864 to early 1868, the newspaper's managing editor was the very radical Belgian astronomer and naturalist Jean-Charles Houzeau. Having a somewhat swarthy complexion, he did nothing to dispel the widespread belief that he was black.*

Though black men had voted before in America, this engraving was aptly captioned "THE FIRST VOTE" when it appeared on the cover of the November 16, 1867, issue of **Harper's Weekly**. It commemorates the first time black men voted in ex-CSA states in significant numbers. "Every one of the several Southern States which have voted under the reconstruction acts of Congress have been carried by the white and colored loyalists," the newspaper reported. "Louisiana, Virginia, Alabama, and now Georgia have declared by large majorities of Union men in favor of Conventions to remodel the State Constitutions on the basis of equal rights to all, and in each and all of them positive and decided Unionists of both colors have been chosen to assist in this labor of remodeling the State laws." With his striking representation of an elder artisan, probable entrepreneur, and soldier, Alfred Waud suggests the range of black men who cherished the right to vote.

Several hundred of these public servants had been enslaved for some, if not all, of their lives. Others, like George Ruby, president of Texas's Union League and state senator in the early 1870s, never were. And there were mystery men like the driven, clearly learned Robert Elliott, who appeared in Charleston, South Carolina, in 1867 and became associate editor of the *South Carolina Leader*, mottoed "Equality and Union." His involvement in politics resulted in his becoming one of the first black congressmen.

These post-bellum black lawmakers and law keepers reflected range in education as well. The once enslaved Abram Colby, a Georgia state legislator,

From the February 15, 1868, issue of **Frank Leslie's Illustrated Newspaper**: *delegates at work during Virginia's constitutional convention in Richmond (December 1867–April 1868). The new state constitution gave black men the right to vote and hold some offices. It also mandated public schools for black and white children. About 70 percent of the 105 delegates were Republicans, about 20 percent black.*

was illiterate—"I make [my son] read all my letters and do all my writings." But more than 80 percent of the black men who held office could read and write. More than a few had graduated from a college or university. Examples include New York City–born South Carolina state legislator (1868–1873) Benjamin Boseman (Maine Medical School); Philadelphia-born Florida secretary of state (1869–1873) Reverend Jonathan Gibbs (Dartmouth College); and his brother, also a minister, Mifflin Gibbs (Oberlin Law School), a municipal judge (1873–1875) in Little Rock, Arkansas. Whatever their prewar status and level of education, whether laborers or entrepreneurs, many of these men had history in the freedom crusade: they had worked on the Underground Railroad, operated secret schools, raised money for the antislavery cause, or served in the Union armed forces.

Most early histories of Reconstruction portrayed black and white Republicans in the South as fools or cheats. Today's scholars agree that while

Pennsylvania-born William James Whipper, nephew of the William Whipper who was part of the Downing-Douglass delegation that met with President Johnson in 1866. When the war started, the younger Whipper was practicing law in Ohio. He joined the Union Army in spring 1864. After the war, he settled in South Carolina. There, his enterprises included a rice plantation on Hilton Head Island and a law office in Columbia. Whipper was also a member of the South Carolina legislature (1868–1872, 1875–1876). He and Frances Rollin married in September 1868. Some contend that her book on Martin Delany only got published because she used her nickname, Frank.

some were ill equipped or corrupt (as were some Democrats), most did their jobs and a lot of good, from pursuing social change (such as desegregation of streetcars) to taking care of everyday business: arresting criminals, collecting taxes, running post offices, overseeing the construction of schools. Mothers, wives, sisters, and daughters cheered them on, believing—and here and there seeing—that good things would accrue to them, too, from the progress of their men.

Take South Carolina's new constitution, which outlawed debtors' prison and mandated a public school system. It declared that when a woman married, whatever property she had was hers, not her husband's. It also gave women the right to sue for divorce. William Whipper, one of the convention's one hundred and twenty-four delegates (seventy-six of whom were black), had lobbied for women to have the right to vote. "I acknowledge the superiority of women," he said. "Is it right or just to deprive these intelligent beings of the privileges which we enjoy?" This was not surprising from a man soon to wed Frances Rollin, a member of Charleston's black bourgeoisie. Rollin had sued a steamer because its captain had refused to let her travel first-class. Around the time of the South Carolina convention, her labor of love was published: *Life and Public Services of Martin R. Delany.* Whether or not Whipper's fellow conventioneers were dating or married to women with Rollin's brains and steel, not enough of them were ready to be as bold as he. His motion was rejected. Still, women in South Carolina and elsewhere felt they had reason to believe in what poet Frances Harper called that "brighter coming day" in a nation on the verge of radical change.

"THE GREAT OBSTRUCTION"

INDIAN LODGE AT MEDICINE CREEK, KANSAS—SCENE OF THE LATE INDIAN PEACE COUNCIL.—Sketched by J. Howland.—[See Page 725.]

In an 1867 treaty, Arapaho-Cheyenne and Apache-Comanche-Kiowa confederations (roughly seven thousand men, women, and children) released all claim to land beyond their reservations. The U.S. government agreed to build homes and schools for them and provide provisions (food, clothing, medicine) and personnel (teachers, a miller, a blacksmith). The American government did not fully keep its word. This engraving is from the November 16, 1867, issue of **Harper's Weekly**.

The nation was expanding while in the throes of Reconstruction. In April 1867, Congress approved the purchase from Russia of about six hundred thousand square miles of land, long home to Tlingit and other peoples the treaty called "uncivilized native tribes." By the time Russian America became America's Alaska, Nebraska had moved from territory to state and the nation was widening its West.

Secretary of State William Henry Seward (Republican), former New York governor, state senator, and U.S. senator. Seward was a die-hard Manifest Destiny man: like many Americans, he believed that the United States had a divine right to all of North America. Seward was angling for the Alaska purchase before the Civil War. Many mocked it as "Seward's Icebox" or "Seward's Folly." They thought the purchase price of $7.2 million (about two cents an acre) a poor use of taxpayers' money. Seward would be vindicated, but when oil and gold were discovered in his "folly," he was dead.

In October 1867 at Medicine Lodge Creek in Kansas, government officials made a deal with two Native American confederations for their people to move to reservations in Indian Territory. The Native Americans also agreed to let the railroads be: not interfere with any under construction or on the drawing board. The same applied to other construction projects—wagon roads, mail stations—and forts.

Native Americans had not been the only impediment to the Pacific Railroad. There had been mudslides, avalanches, and other natural and man-made disasters. At one point, Central Pacific feared trouble with its "coolies," as racists called Asians, especially unskilled workers. Several Chinese crews, ranked by many as the most diligent and disciplined workers, had gone on strike in June 1867. They wanted a ten-hour workday and a raise from thirty to thirty-five dollars a month—what white laborers made. Instead

Great Plains military posts included Kansas's Fort Leavenworth, first home of the 10th Cavalry. These troopers protected stagecoaches, built forts, and, like other "Buffalo Soldier" outfits and all-white army units, battled Native Americans. This sketch of 10th Cavalrymen by the acclaimed Frederic Remington was one of several that accompanied his article on Buffalo Soldiers in the April 1889 issue of **Century** *magazine.*

From the September 12, 1868, issue of **Frank Leslie's Illustrated Newspaper**, *captioned "THE CAPTURE OF A FREIGHT TRAIN OF THE UNION PACIFIC RAILROAD BY SIOUX INDIANS. ANTICS OF THE SAVAGES AFTER THE CAPTURE." Just as the making of pre–Civil War America involved the death and uprooting of untold numbers of Native Americans, such as the Pequot (Northeast), the Cherokee, Coushatta, and Seminole (Southeast), the Miami and Potawatomi (Midwest), and the Apache, Modoc, and Cayuse (the Southwest and Far West), the nation's postwar growth resulted in the killing and cramping onto reservations of countless indigenous people in the West. Late in life, General Phil Sheridan, who had become a celebrated "Indian fighter," told the flat-footed truth: "We took away their country and their means of support, broke up their mode of living, their habits of life, introduced disease and decay among them, and it was for this and against this that they made war. Could anyone expect less?"*

of compromise, management said there would be no deliveries of food and other necessities into their camps until the men went back to work. The strike was over in about a week. The Chinese got a two-dollar raise.

The Swedish engineer Alfred Nobel patented dynamite that year; Adelia Waldron, the washing machine. Wall Street was enthralled with a new gizmo, the stock ticker. It let investors get stock prices lickety-split. And in August 1867, President Johnson moved fast and furious to strike back at Congressional Reconstruction. He had already pressured several cabinet members who did not condemn Republican Reconstruction initiatives to resign their posts. Secretary of War Edwin Stanton was next.

When asked to resign, Stanton refused. So Johnson suspended him. According to the Tenure of Office Act, the president could do that while Congress was not in session and await the Senate's yea or nay when it reconvened. The president had asked General Grant—who had advised Johnson against suspending Stanton—to be secretary of war in the meantime. Grant accepted the appointment begrudgingly. The president also ignored Grant's counsel against removing General Sheridan as commander of Louisiana and Texas. (By then Sheridan had removed more men from office, including Texas governor James Throckmorton, whom he deemed a hindrance to

Ohio-born Secretary of War Edwin McMasters Stanton. Before holding political office, Stanton was a lawyer in Ohio, Pennsylvania, then D.C. His most famous case was as defense counsel for then-representative Daniel Sickles (a district commander during Congressional Reconstruction). Sickles had shot dead his wife's lover, District Attorney Philip Barton Key (son of Francis Scott Key, composer of "The Star-Spangled Banner"). Stanton got Sickles off on what was then a new defense: temporary insanity.

Reconstruction.) After Sheridan, the president removed General Dan Sickles as commander of the Carolinas.

"What in God's name has gotten into Johnson?" one of the president's supporters wrote another in August 1867. Did the president not know that his actions might push more moderate Republicans into the radical camp and escalate the war between him and Congress? Andy Johnson believed he had more white people on his side. His opposition to the Fourteenth Amendment and the whole of Congressional Reconstruction—his racism—had in fact earned him more white supporters, and not only in the South. He was confident that his rise in popularity would result in victories for Democrats in upcoming local and state elections outside the South. As the Democratic Party's star rose, the Republicans would be muzzled, he was sure.

In these elections, Republicans finally dealt with the longstanding charge that they were a bunch of hypocrites. Where was their zeal for black male suffrage outside of the ex-CSA states? For example, black men could vote in only a handful of Northern states: New York and the New England states except for Connecticut. Some of these states had restrictions. In New York, a black man had to have property valued at no less than two hundred and fifty dollars. Massachusetts had a literacy requirement, but it was not limited to blacks. It had been added in 1857 to keep immigrants, especially the Irish, from voting.

Only a few white Republicans had been for black male suffrage throughout America before the war. In 1867, most Republicans running for office (from alderman to governor) in the North made black male suffrage a campaign issue. Some did it for face-saving reasons, some from a sense of fair play. And some paid a political price.

"FATHERS, SAVE US FROM NEGRO EQUALITY." These words were printed on banners held aloft by little white girls dressed in white as they were wagoned around Ohio towns. Most of the "fathers" voted Democratic. One exception was the governor's race: Rutherford Hayes, a Republican, had a slim victory.

Democrats had big victories in Thad Stevens's Pennsylvania. "Rebels are very jubilant over the result of the elections in Ohio and Pennsylvania," lamented John Bowles, a Republican in Georgia, in a letter to Ohio representative Samuel Shellabarger. According to Bowles, the rebels were in a fever for the day when, as they put it, "all Yankees and white niggers will have to leave the South." Democrat victories in New York and New Jersey added to the rebels' delight.

President Johnson whipped up more resistance to Congressional Reconstruction in his December 3, 1867, Annual Message to Congress (today's State of the Union address). As required, he reported on a range of matters, including troop strength (about 56,000); expenditures for the navy (about $31 million); the national debt (about $2.7 billion); and the number of patents and designs registered (11,655).

Before all this, the president lit into Congressional Reconstruction. He said he would not be doing his job if he did not "recommend the repeal of the acts of Congress which place ten of the Southern States under the domination of military masters." Letting black men vote and participate in government was calamitous, he claimed. None of the "dangers" the nation had ever faced were as great as those that would result from the effort "to Africanize the half of our country," he charged.

Thad Stevens had gone from calling Andy Johnson a damn scoundrel to declaring him "the great obstruction." For Congressional Reconstruction to succeed, Johnson needed to be knocked out of the way, Stevens and others believed.

"IMPEACHMENT—THE GUARD BEFORE THE WAR OFFICE," from the March 14, 1868, issue of **Harper's Weekly**. This was the Seventeenth Street entrance of Secretary of War Stanton's headquarters. The War Office's Pennsylvania Avenue entrance was a short walk away from the Executive Mansion. Along with several other military institutions, the War Department became part of the Department of Defense in the 1940s. The War Office site became part of what is today the Eisenhower Executive Office Building.

The only legal way to end Johnson's presidency was laid out in Article II of the Constitution: "The President, Vice President and all civil Officers of the United States, shall be removed from office on Impeachment for, and Conviction of, Treason, Bribery, or other high Crimes and Misdemeanors."

Only a legislative body can impeach (indict). In the case of the president, it is the U.S. House of Representatives, where impeachment requires a simple majority (say, 51–49). If impeached, Johnson would face trial in the U.S. Senate, where conviction requires at least a two-thirds majority. Since the nation's founding, no president had ever been impeached, let alone convicted.

The call to impeach Andy Johnson had been in the wind awhile. "We believe . . . that the President should be impeached for high treason," bellowed the *Chicago Tribune* in March 1866. Months later, a correspondent for the *Christian Recorder* said, Amen: "A greater reprobate, and, consequently, more unworthy being, never filled the presidential chair."

Radicals in Congress had long been eager to impeach Johnson. There was snooping into his finances. Had all those pardons been for a price? And did he have a soft spot for Jeff Davis? Johnson had once sent someone to Fort Monroe to make sure Davis was not being abused, and he had not objected to the shifting of Davis's trial from a military tribunal to a civilian court. If not for that, Davis would not have been released on $100,000 bail in May 1867. (To the horror of many Northerners, eccentric newspaperman Horace Greeley and industrialist Cornelius Vanderbilt, both New Yorkers, were among the people who posted bond for Jeff Davis.) After all the digging to find *something* on which to hang Andy Johnson—*nothing*. Then his suspension of Stanton and reassigning of Generals Sheridan and Sickles had many in Congress in impeachment fever again.

On January 12, 1868, by a huge majority, the Senate voted "no" on Stanton's suspension. Anticipating that, Johnson had asked Grant not to surrender the keys to the War Office when the verdict came back. The president was convinced that the Tenure of Office Act was unconstitutional. He wanted a fight, a way to create a court case to prove his point. Grant wanted no part of Johnson's drama. On January 13, he turned in the keys, torpedoing the cordial relationship he and Johnson once had. Grant inched closer to the radical camp.

About a month later, the president sent Stanton a letter informing him that he was not suspended, but fired. Johnson then informed the Senate of what he had done "by virtue of the power and authority vested in the President by the Constitution and the laws of the United States." Several senators made a beeline for Stanton's office to urge him to defy the president. And that's just what Stanton did: he locked himself in his office. Messages of support flooded in. The most famous one came from the usually verbose radical Massachusetts senator Charles Sumner: "Stick."

When word hit the House—"Didn't I tell you so?" crowed Thad Stevens, seventy-six and ailing. "If you don't kill the beast, it will kill you." Moderate

Republicans (the majority) joined with radicals past ready to get rid of "the great obstruction." On February 24, the House voted to impeach the president. The yeas were 128, the nays 47.

There were eleven articles of impeachment. Nine charges pertained to alleged violations of the Tenure of Office Act in the Stanton affair. The tenth article charged the president with slandering and disrespecting Congress. Johnson's wild remarks during his 1866 "swing around the circle" tour constituted some of the supporting evidence. The eleventh article was essentially all the charges in one. It claimed that Johnson's violation of the Tenure of Office Act and his attacks on Congressional Reconstruction amounted to a conspiracy to invalidate Congress. Two charges were designated "high crime," the rest, "high misdemeanor." There were rumblings of another civil war. Newspapers did brisk business.

What were the chances that the Senate would convict the president? Slim, some argued. Johnson had not *appointed* Stanton; he had inherited him from Lincoln. As for saying vicious things about Congress, as Johnson's defense team would argue, didn't the president have a right to free speech? But Republicans had a majority in the Senate. Would they "stick"? Then again, there was the Ben Wade factor.

Wade was the Senate's president *pro tem* (short for the Latin *pro tempore,* "for the time being"), the person who presides over it when its rightful chair, the vice president, can't be there. (And back then, when a vice president replaced a president, as Andy Johnson had, the vice presidency remained vacant until the next presidential election.) If Johnson was convicted, the Senate's president *pro tem* would become the nation's president, according to the rules of succession at the time. Wade was way too radical for some of his Republican colleagues. The senator from Ohio was for black empowerment *and* women's suffrage. More troubling still for captains of industry, big supporters of the Republican Party, Wade had issues with capitalism and wished unions well as a counterweight to Big

Members of the House of Representatives who served as the prosecution team ("house managers") in President Johnson's trial. Only two of them were moderates: John Armor Bingham (Ohio) and James Falconer Wilson (Iowa). Like Thaddeus Stevens and George Boutwell, the rest were radicals: Thomas Williams (Pennsylvania); John Alexander Logan (Illinois), "father" of what became Memorial Day; and Benjamin Franklin Butler (Massachusetts), a former proslavery Democrat who had raised a black regiment. Many white Southerners reviled Butler as "The Beast" because when he was military governor of Louisiana, he was fierce. His draconian actions included having a man hanged for ripping down an American flag.

"THE COMMITTEE OF MANAGERS OF THE HOUSE OF REPRESENTATIVES"
(back row, left to right) James Wilson, George Boutwell, John Logan; (front row, left to right) Benjamin Butler, Thaddeus Stevens, Thomas Williams, John Bingham

Business. Wade was also for land reform: moving more of it out of the hands of the minority (the wealthy) and into the hands of the majority (working- and middle-class folk). He had received the applause of one of the people blamed for uprisings against the aristocracy in Europe in the late 1840s: Karl Marx, co-author of the *Communist Manifesto*, co-founder of the International Workingmen's Association, and archenemy of capitalists everywhere. With Johnson's term up in eight months, some Republicans began to wonder if it wouldn't be wiser to endure "the great obstruction" than to elevate Ben Wade to the presidency.

The High Court of Impeachment commenced on March 5, 1868, with the swearing in of the senators and Supreme Court Chief Justice Salmon Chase presiding. After hours upon days upon weeks of speeches by the prosecution team and Johnson's lawyers, on May 16, it was time for the Senate to vote. First up, article eleven. The charge was read aloud; the roll call began with Rhode Island senator Henry Anthony (Republican).

67

The High Court of Impeachment in session on Monday, March 23, 1868, based on an engraving in the April 11, 1868, issue of **Frank Leslie's Illustrated Newspaper**.

Tickets to the impeachment trial were a hot commodity.

"Mr. Senator Anthony, how say you?" asked Chief Justice Chase. "Is the respondent, Andrew Johnson, President of the United States, guilty, or not guilty, of a high misdemeanor as charged in this article of impeachment?"

"Guilty!"

Fifty-three more senators to go: Democrat James Bayard, Jr., from Delaware—*Not guilty!* . . . Republican Roscoe Conkling from New York—*Guilty!* . . . Republican James Doolittle from Wisconsin—*Not guilty!* . . . Republican Frederick Frelinghuysen from New Jersey—*Guilty!* . . . Democrat Thomas Hendricks from Indiana—*Not guilty!* . . . Republican John Sherman from Ohio—*Guilty!* . . . Republican Charles Sumner from Massachusetts—*Guilty!* . . . Republican Lyman Trumbull from Illinois—*Not guilty!*

Acquittal required nineteen "not guilty" votes. When George Vickers,

Democrat from Maryland, was called, the vote was 30 (guilty) to 18 (not guilty). When Vickers voted—*Not guilty!*—it didn't matter that the remaining five senators would vote "Guilty!" The Republicans had failed to "stick." Seven had voted "not guilty," so President Johnson was acquitted on the eleventh charge. Thad Stevens, too weak to walk, had to be carried out of the Senate chamber. To the shout "What was the verdict?" he replied, "The country is going to the devil!"

The trial adjourned until May 26 because of the upcoming Republican National Convention. When it resumed, senators voted on two more articles. Both times—acquittal. Just as

Senator Lyman Trumbull, author of the 1866 Freedmen's Bureau and civil rights bills, was one of the Republicans who voted for acquittal. He did so "governed by what my reason and judgment tell me is the truth, and the justice and the law of this case." Trumbull thought it a grave mistake to oust a president because the majority of Congress hated him and his policies. "[N]o future President will be safe who happens to differ with a majority of the House and two-thirds of the Senate on any measure deemed by them important, particularly if of a political character."

before, the vote was 35 to 19. The same seven Republicans voted "not guilty." Because there was every reason to believe they would vote the same way on the remaining articles, the Senate decided to end the trial then and there. Later that day, Secretary of War Edwin Stanton resigned.

With the news of Johnson's acquittal, gun salutes and fireworks made a festival of Southern skies. Where rejoicing ratcheted up into violence, some Republicans went into hiding; others left town. "It is impossible to paint in true colors the woeful condition of Union men in the South," wrote a Republican in Alabama to Representative Elihu Washburne of Illinois. Washburne received an equally disturbing letter from a Florida Republican: "News of the failure to convict Johnson will be like Greek fire throughout the entire South. May God save our country from the consuming conflagration. The eyes of the rebels sparkle like those of the fiery serpent. They hope they have found their 'lost cause.'"

This 1868 Currier & Ives lithograph lampoons the prosecution team in the impeachment trial. Mounting another attempt to remove President Johnson from office would be beating a dead horse, it warns.

While Democrats rejoiced over Johnson's acquittal, Republicans in Congress kept the faith that they would prevail in controlling the government. They had lost the battle to oust the president, but they would win the Fourteenth Amendment.

In June 1868, Congress was ready to readmit Arkansas. Congress had approved the state's new constitution and the Bowie State had ratified the Fourteenth Amendment. President Johnson vetoed the bill to readmit

Arkansas. He reasoned that if he didn't, he'd be implicitly endorsing the Reconstruction acts. A few hours after his veto, from the House came: "*Resolved*, That the said bill do pass, two thirds of the House of Representatives agreeing to pass the same." Two days later, the Senate concurred—"the bill do pass." Arkansas was back in the Union. A few days after that, Congress had a bill to readmit Alabama, Florida, Georgia, Louisiana, North Carolina, and South Carolina as soon as they ratified the Fourteenth Amendment (Florida had already done so on June 9).

Some South Carolinians had sent Congress a petition "on behalf of The White People of South Carolina," protesting the new state constitution as "the work of Northern adventurers, Southern renegades and ignorant negroes," and claiming it established "in this State negro supremacy," given the state's majority black population. The Palmetto State petitioners embraced a duty to the "proud Caucasian race, whose sovereignty on earth God has ordained." False and flawed interpretations of the Holy Bible had a lot to do with why some whites believed they had a divine right to rule. Many white supremacists actually believed they were "good Christians." This included members of the KKK.

And what of the "negro supremacy" the South Carolinians feared? Whites had practically all the wealth (including land) in South Carolina. What's more, there was no black movement to rule supremely and vindictively over whites. For sure, there were blacks who had no love for whites. There were instances of "Ole Massa's" barn getting torched and of a wild bunch knifing a Johnny Reb on a lonely road. But the wholesale black desire was for *living free and equal*, not payback. Congress ignored the petition.

Johnson swiftly vetoed the bill to readmit South Carolina and five other states. Within hours, on June 25, both houses of Congress had resolved that the "bill do pass." By late July, all six states had ratified the Fourteenth Amendment, as had twenty-one other states by then. With the three-fourths requirement met, on July 28, 1868, Secretary of State Seward certified that the Fourteenth Amendment was part of the Constitution.

On the very day Georgia was readmitted to the Union (July 25), shortly before the Fourteenth Amendment became law, a motion in its legislature portended things to come. White legislators wanted to oust Abram Colby and more than two dozen other black legislators. The whites argued that because the state's constitution did not explicitly say blacks could hold office, they should not.

Scoundrels! No doubt that's what Thad Stevens would have called Georgia's white legislators. But by then Stevens was a whisper. Between one

Fourteenth Amendment

Section 1. All persons born or naturalized in the United States and subject to the jurisdiction thereof, are citizens of the United States and of the State wherein they reside. No State shall make or enforce any law which shall abridge the privileges or immunities of citizens of the United States; nor shall any State deprive any person of life, liberty, or property, without due process of law; nor deny to any person within its jurisdiction the equal protection of the laws.

Section 2. Representatives shall be apportioned among the several States according to their respective numbers, counting the whole number of persons in each State, excluding Indians not taxed. But when the right to vote at any election for the choice of electors for President and Vice President of the United States, Representatives in Congress, the Executive and Judicial officers of a State, or the members of the Legislature thereof, is denied to any of the male inhabitants of such State, being twenty-one years of age, and citizens of the United States, or in any way abridged, except for participation in rebellion, or other crime, the basis of representation therein shall be reduced in the proportion which the number of such male citizens shall bear to the whole number of male citizens twenty-one years of age in such State.

Section 3. No person shall be a Senator or Representative in Congress, or elector of President and Vice President, or hold any office, civil or military, under the United States, or under any State, who, having previously taken an oath, as a member of Congress, or as an officer of the United States, or as a member of any State legislature, or as an executive or judicial officer of any State, to support the Constitution of the United States, shall have engaged in insurrection or rebellion against the same, or given aid or comfort to the enemies thereof. But Congress may by a vote of two-thirds of each House, remove such disability.

Section 4. The validity of the public debt of the United States, authorized by law, including debts incurred for payment of pensions and bounties for services in suppressing insurrection or rebellion, shall not be questioned. But neither the United States nor any State shall assume or pay any debt or obligation incurred in aid of insurrection or rebellion against the United

States, or any claim for the loss or emancipation of any slave; but all such debts, obligations and claims shall be held illegal and void.

<u>Section 5</u>. The Congress shall have power to enforce, by appropriate legislation, the provisions of this article.

The Fourteenth Amendment cemented black citizenship (Section 1); tied a state's representation in Congress to the number of men allowed to vote (Section 2); banned thousands of Southerners from holding office (Section 3); and dashed any hope of war-related debt relief and reimbursement to former slaveholders for the people the federal government had freed (Section 4). The amendment infuriated many women because Section 2 carried no penalty for denying women the vote. Those women (a vocal minority) had put their push for suffrage on the back burner to press for the abolition of slavery. They had been led to believe that once that occurred, a unified movement for black and women's suffrage would ensue.

day and the next, at midnight on August 11, he died. He was buried in Lancaster, Pennsylvania, in a cemetery that did not discriminate based on religion or race. His epitaph: "I repose in this quiet and secluded spot, not from any natural preference for solitude, but, finding other cemeteries limited by charter rules as to race, I have chosen this, that I might illustrate in my death the principles which I advocated through a long life—Equality of Man before his Creator."

A few weeks after Stevens died, the Georgia legislature followed through on expelling its black members. The fact that white moderate Republicans (the majority) supported the expulsion made it an even more bitter pill for Abram Colby and his black colleagues. But the black men would be reinstated under orders from Congress, and with the support of the president. That president was not Andy Johnson.

Ousted Georgia legislator Tunis G. Campbell, Sr. Born in New Jersey, he spent much of his early life in New York City. There, he became an AME Zion Church minister and supported his family as a hotel steward, then with the bakery he co-owned. In 1863, Tunis Campbell went south, to the region that had been designated for blacks under General Sherman's Special Field Order No. 15. As an employee of the Freedmen's Bureau, Campbell helped blacks on the Georgia Sea Islands build up. His goal was to establish an independent republic. The Freedmen's Bureau fired him in 1866. When Campbell moved to mainland Georgia, he became a leader in McIntosh County, population about five thousand, with blacks outnumbering whites almost three to one. When he was elected to Georgia's senate in 1868, his son, Tunis G. Campbell, Jr., was elected to its house.

"THE BODY OF THADDEUS STEVENS LYING IN STATE AT THE CAPITOL," from the cover of the August 29, 1868, issue of **Harper's Weekly**. The honor guard was composed of black Zouaves, so called because the volunteer regiment's uniforms echoed those of French Zouaves (bolero jacket, pantaloons, white leggings). About six thousand people paid their respects to Stevens in the rotunda of the Capitol Building. Elsewhere, near and far, others whooped it up. "The prayers of the righteous have at last removed the congressional curse!" began the item *"THAD STEVENS IS DEAD"* in a mid-August 1868 issue of **The Planters' Banner**, a Louisiana newspaper.

Though not a radical, Grant supported the First Reconstruction Act, and Congressional Reconstruction was the Republican Party's primary plank in 1868. Grant's running mate, Indiana representative Schuyler "The Smiler" Colfax, had been speaker of the House since 1863. He became Ben Wade's nephew-in-law shortly after the election.

Back in May 1868, at its national convention in Chicago, Illinois, the Republican Party picked the Hero of Appomattox as its presidential candidate. General Grant officially accepted in a letter that began, "If elected to the office of the President of the United States, it will be my endeavor to administer all the laws in good faith, with economy, and with the view of giving peace, quiet, and protection everywhere." His closing words became his

The overthrow of Congressional Reconstruction was the cornerstone of the Democratic Party's campaign. Its presidential candidate, Horatio Seymour, had opposed the Emancipation Proclamation and the Fourteenth Amendment. His critics made hay of the scuttlebutt that during New York City's horrendous draft riots of July 1863, then–New York governor Seymour had addressed a crowd of white rowdies as "my friends." Seymour's running mate, Francis Preston Blair, Jr.—Democrat-turned-Republican-turned-Democrat—was a former Missouri representative and Union Army veteran. Blair's rebel-rousing speeches during the campaign caused many fence-sitters in the North to vote for the Grant-Colfax ticket.

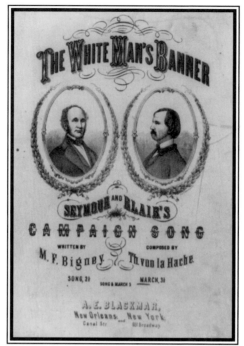

campaign slogan: "Let us have peace."

"This is a White Man's Country; Let White Men Rule" declared a campaign badge for the Democratic Party's presidential and vice presidential candidates, Horatio Seymour and Frank Blair. Andy Johnson had hoped for the nomination, but Democratic Party bosses, though happy he had been acquitted of impeachment charges, deemed him too controversial. They wanted to move on. Democrats did not, however, move up into power. Ulysses S. Grant won.

A few days before Grant's inauguration, in late February 1869, Congress was ready to submit to the states for ratification a fifteenth amendment to the Constitution. Its whole point was to give black men the right to vote nationally. Some Republicans supported the amendment on moral grounds; for others it was politics: they wanted to enlarge the Republican voting bloc. As Reverend John Peck of Pittsburgh said of the amendment, "The Republican Party had done [us] good but they were doing themselves good at the same time." For Mississippi, Virginia, and Texas, still out of the Union because they had failed to either ratify the Fourteenth Amendment or produce an acceptable constitution, Congress made ratification of the Fifteenth Amendment an added requirement for readmission.

Before March 1869 was out, seven states in the North had ratified the Fifteenth Amendment; in the South, five. *Whoa!* cried some women's rights activists. Elizabeth Cady Stanton, who had crusaded for the abolition of slavery and who had called Fred Douglass and other blacks "friend," revealed in her fury over the amendment that she was not immune to racism. "Think of Patrick and Sambo and Hans and Yung Tung, who do not know the difference between a monarchy and a republic, who cannot read the Declaration of Independence . . . making laws for . . . [white] women of wealth and education," she snapped in a sweeping attack on Irish, black, German, and Chinese men as ignoramuses. She said this at a January 1869 women's suffrage convention.

The Fifteenth Amendment was the subject of great debate at the mid-May 1869 convention of the American Equal Rights Association (AERA), which formed in 1866 and claimed to be about securing equal rights for *all* Americans, especially the right to vote.

At the 1869 AERA convention in New York City, Fred Douglass insisted that black male suffrage had to be the top priority. "With us, the matter is a question of life and death," he said. "When women, because they are women, are hunted down through the cities of New York and New Orleans; when they are dragged from their houses and hung upon lamp-posts; when their children are torn from their arms, and their brains dashed out upon the pavement; when they are objects of insult and outrage at every turn; when they are in danger of having their homes burnt down over their heads; when their children are not allowed to enter schools; then they will have an urgency to obtain the ballot equal to our own."

When someone shouted out, "Is that not all true about black women?" Douglass replied, "Yes, yes, yes; it is true of the black woman, but not because she is a woman, but because she is black."

Susan Anthony weighed in that people who thought as Douglass did had their priorities out of order. If the "whole loaf" of suffrage was not to be had, then it should be given first to the most "intelligent" and "capable" women. Frances Harper and Lucy Stone were among the women who sided with Douglass. The AERA was torn asunder. Friendships blew up. Stanton and Anthony founded the New York City–based and all-women-led National Woman Suffrage Association. It campaigned for a "whole loaf" amendment and rejection of the Fifteenth Amendment. Lucy Stone and others started the Boston-based American Woman Suffrage Association to crusade for

These leading white women's rights activists had contributed their time, talent, and treasure to the antislavery movement. Clockwise, from top: Lucretia Mott, first president of the AERA; Elizabeth Cady Stanton (no relation to Edwin Stanton), who co-organized, with Mott, the 1848 women's rights convention in Seneca Falls, New York; Mary Ashton Rice Livermore, co-founder of the U.S. Sanitary Commission (the Civil War's equivalent to the Red Cross); Lydia Maria Child, prolific writer and editor, whose least political creation is her best known: the poem that begins "Over the river and through the woods to Grandmother's house we go"; Susan Brownlow Anthony, whose other causes included an eight-hour workday; and Grace Greenwood, the pen name of poet and journalist Sara Jane Clarke Lippincott. Center: Anna Elizabeth Dickinson. She started her activism as a teenager and gained fame as a terrific orator during the Civil War for her pro-Republican, get-out-the-vote speaking tours in the Northeast.

*Philadelphia-based Frances Ellen Watkins Harper was the most celebrated black writer of the nineteenth century—poems, essays, short stories, novels—and was called the "Bronze Muse." Among her best-known works is the novel **Iola Leroy; Or, Shadows Uplifted** (1892), about a woman who teaches school and in other ways contributes to the uplift of blacks during Reconstruction after she discovers that she is not white, as she was raised. Before the war, Harper was a much sought-after speaker on the antislavery lecture circuit. After the war, she took her oratorical skills south to recruit and bolster existing "soldiers" in the civil rights crusade. Not all black women sided with Douglass on the Fifteenth Amendment, as Harper did. Sojourner Truth was among those who sided with Stanton and Anthony.*

Massachusetts-born Lucy Stone was one of the few women to attend college before the Civil War. She had to work for several years, mostly as a teacher, to save up money for it. Her father, a prosperous farmer and tanner, refused to fund her dream, though he had been happy to foot the bill for her brothers' education. After she graduated from Ohio's Oberlin College (1847) at age twenty-nine, Stone became a lecturer for the American Anti-Slavery Society. In 1850, she spearheaded the first national women's rights convention (Worcester, Massachusetts). When Stone married, she did not take her husband's surname and caused quite a stir.

women's suffrage while supporting the half loaf.

Amid the political dramas, one thing people of various political persuasions could celebrate was "the wedding of the rails" on May 10, 1869, after years of hard, dangerous work and setbacks from late and lost supplies, natural disasters, bridge collapses, deaths from bad blasts, Native American attacks, barroom fights on days off, dysentery, falls from cliffs, and freight train wrecks. When Union Pacific and Central Pacific track connected at Promontory Point, Utah, church bells chimed, cannons boomed, and brass bands blared as the news whipped around telegraph wires. "EAST AND WEST. Completion of the Great Line Spanning the Continent," trumpeted the *New York Times* front-page story the next day.

*New towns sprang up around the railroad's path. Among them were Reno, Nevada; Fresno, California; and Cheyenne and Laramie in the nation's youngest organized territory, Wyoming, created by Congress in July 1868. (Wyoming made history seven months after the "wedding of the rails" when it granted women the vote.) New and burgeoning towns and cities in the West would aid the federal government's goal to displace more Native Americans. This engraving was captioned "WORK ON THE LAST MILE OF THE PACIFIC RAILROAD—MINGLING OF EUROPEAN WITH ASIATIC LABORERS" when it appeared in the May 29, 1869, issue of **Harper's Weekly**. Although the newspaper considered itself enlightened, it often ran drawings with grotesque depictions of Chinese and Irish people, usually the former as sly foxes and the latter as apes.*

The nation's first transcontinental railroad promised increased commerce between Asia and Europe, increased import and export business for American companies, more freight business for railroads, and more orders for steel mills, iron foundries, and other enterprises that dealt in railroad-related goods and

"INTERIOR OF A PALACE HOTEL CAR USED ON THE PACIFIC RAILROAD," from the May 29, 1869, issue of **Harper's Weekly**. "These cars have all the accommodations of a first-class steamer," the newspaper reported. "The passenger from Chicago to San Francisco will take a state-room, go to bed at midnight, and have breakfast, dinner, and supper on board the train while flying across the continent." In contrast to the wagon route, crossing the plains by train cost under two hundred dollars and took only days.

services. People saw nothing but prosperity ahead. Ironically, four months after the Promontory Point jubilee came loss and panic in the stock market.

Financiers Jay Gould and Jim Fisk had manipulated the price of gold. They gobbled it up to drive up the price, with plans to sell high—make a killing. But President Grant smelled a rat. His secretary of the treasury, former representative George Boutwell, put $4 million in government gold onto the market on September 24, 1869, on Grant's orders. This caused the price of gold to drop, putting an end to the Gould-Fisk scheme, but also putting a hole in the pockets of people who had invested in gold when its price was high. Grant's stock went down, too. People knew he was chummy with Gould and Fisk, and some wondered if he had been in on the scheme. (He hadn't.)

Gould and Fisk were not anomalies. Greed was as rampant as ever in America, with growing corporate control of major industries, from banking and railroads to coal mines. The more powerful the corporations became, the worse the lot of their low-level employees and the greater the number of brakemen, carpenters, miners, and other workers who joined labor unions. The largest one was the National Labor Union (NLU), a coalition of white agricultural and industrial workers' unions. An eight-hour workday was the number one item on the NLU's agenda at a time when many people were forced to work ten or more hours a day. Labor's (workers') other grievances against capital (Big Business) included low wages and unsafe working conditions.

Isaac Myers of Baltimore, Maryland, was one of a handful of blacks at the NLU's August 1869 convention. "I speak today for the colored men of the whole country," said Myers, co-founder of a ship repair and building business and a caulkers' union. He urged white workers to join forces with black workers and create a more muscular labor organization. But skin color trumped common cause: the NLU wanted no union with blacks. In response, Myers and about two hundred other black laborites from around the nation gathered in D.C.

Millionaire Cornelius Vanderbilt, born poor on what is today New York City's Staten Island. "I have been insane on the subject of moneymaking all my life," he once said. Vanderbilt's first enterprise, at age sixteen, was a ferry service from his island to Manhattan. By the mid-1840s, he had a swift, safe line of steamboats with various East Coast routes. He later went into the luxury-liner and railroad business. By the early 1870s, his empire included New York Central Railroad, a network of lines in the Northeast that went as far as Chicago, Illinois. Its hub was Grand Central Station. Vanderbilt's greatest act of charity was a gift of $1 million in 1873 to a school in the South: today's Vanderbilt University in Nashville, Tennessee. Vanderbilt hoped his gesture would "contribute to strengthening the ties that should exist between all sections of our common country."

and formed the Colored National Labor Union (CNLU). Isaac Myers was president, George Downing vice president, and Lewis Douglass secretary. "In our organization we make no discrimination as to nationality, sex, or color," proclaimed the CNLU manifesto of December 6, 1869.

By then many eyes were on Georgia. In addition to expelling its black members, the Georgia legislature had flouted the Fourteenth Amendment's prohibition on certain ex-Confederates holding office. What's more, the KKK was on the warpath. Abram Colby, one of the ousted black legislators, had been a target. On an autumn evening in 1869, about thirty Klansmen snatched Colby into the woods near his home in Greene County, where blacks outnumbered whites by about two to one. When asked how he'd vote from here on out, figuring they'd "kill me anyhow," he affirmed his loyalty to the Republican Party.

Abram Colby knew who his attackers were: many were farmers, one a lawyer, another a doctor. They whipped Colby before they asked how he'd vote. After his reply, they beat him some more. "The worst thing about the whole matter was this: My mother, wife, and daughter were in the room when they came and carried me out." When Colby's little girl begged the men not to take her daddy away, they pulled a gun on the child "and actually frightened her to death. She never got over it until she died."

Because of violence and the Georgia legislature's defiance, Congress heeded Republican governor Rufus Bullock's request to put Georgia under martial law in early December 1869. Only after its legislature toed the line on the Fourteenth Amendment, reinstated the black legislators, and ratified the Fifteenth Amendment could it rejoin the Union.

The next year brought defeat for women's rights activists who denounced the half-loaf suffrage amendment. By the end of March 1870, having finally met the requirements for readmission, Virginia, Mississippi, and Texas were back in the Union. The three states joined the twenty-six others that had already ratified the Fifteenth Amendment. On March 30, 1870, Grant's secretary of state, Hamilton Fish, certified that it was part of the Constitution.

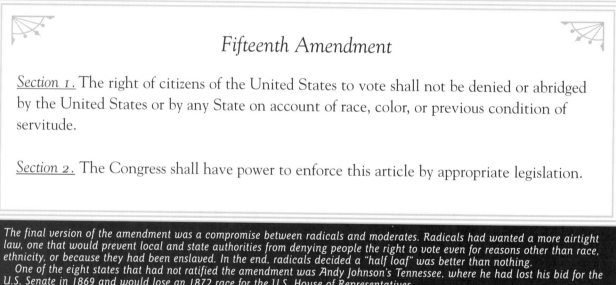

Fifteenth Amendment

<u>Section 1.</u> The right of citizens of the United States to vote shall not be denied or abridged by the United States or by any State on account of race, color, or previous condition of servitude.

<u>Section 2.</u> The Congress shall have power to enforce this article by appropriate legislation.

The final version of the amendment was a compromise between radicals and moderates. Radicals had wanted a more airtight law, one that would prevent local and state authorities from denying people the right to vote even for reasons other than race, ethnicity, or because they had been enslaved. In the end, radicals decided a "half loaf" was better than nothing.

One of the eight states that had not ratified the amendment was Andy Johnson's Tennessee, where he had lost his bid for the U.S. Senate in 1869 and would lose an 1872 race for the U.S. House of Representatives.

A few months after the Fifteenth Amendment became law, Georgia satisfied the requirements for readmission. On July 15, 1870, the Peach State was for the second time readmitted to the Union. Five years after the Civil War ended, all eleven ex-CSA states were back in the Union, with many Republicans in positions of high authority.

All around the South, plantations were producing cotton and other crops. Homes and shops had been built back up. Carpenters were crafting chifforobes and rocking chairs; blacksmiths were fashioning fences and gates.

Many general stores were stocked with everything from crockery, kerosene, and cornmeal to corset stays and bolts of calico. Popular pastimes included attending a baseball game, a county fair, or a circus-come-to-town. And while the well-to-do waltzed, workaday folks did the do-si-do.

This lithograph, "THE FIFTEENTH AMENDMENT AND ITS RESULTS," celebrates black aspirations and people blacks lionized. Among them are the long-bearded John Brown (top right), father of the failed 1859 uprising against slaveholders. Next to Brown is a Radical Republican, Judge Hugh Lenox Bond of Maryland. Opposite Frederick Douglass (bottom left) is AME minister Hiram Rhoades Revels, the first black member of the U.S. Senate. During the war, Revels raised two regiments in Baltimore, Maryland, and served as chaplain of another in Vicksburg, Mississippi, the state he made home. He took his Senate seat in February 1870. It was the seat Jeff Davis had vacated when he threw in with the Confederacy. The scene in the center panel is an example of how blacks celebrated the Fifteenth Amendment. Along with parades, there were pageants and picnics—as there were for black liberation celebrations. Out of Texas came Juneteenth, remembering June 19, 1865, the day the Union general Gordon Granger announced that slavery, like the war, was over. For most blacks, the main date for Freedom Day celebrations was January 1, the day the Emancipation Proclamation went into effect.

As for the cries of "Hang Jeff Davis!"—that had not and would not happen. After much foot-dragging and legal wrangling, his case had been dismissed in early 1869, as were those of about thirty other former high-ranking Confederates. Not Jeff Davis, not Alexander Stephens, not Robert E. Lee—not one leading ex-Confederate paid the ultimate price for treason at the hands of the federal government.

Still there was no peace.

"TWO MEMBERS OF THE KU-KLUX KLAN IN THEIR DISGUISES," from the December 19, 1868, issue of **Harper's Weekly**. Questions posed to candidates for KKK membership included "Did you belong to the Federal army during the late war, and fight against the South during the existence of the same?" and "Are you opposed to negro equality, both social and political?" It is widely believed that the heart of the group's name derived from the Greek word for "circle": **kyklos**. Costumes served to conceal identities and, early on, to frighten superstitious people into thinking the marauders were ghosts of CSA soldiers.

The KKK stayed on the warpath, giving peace no chance. Not only in Georgia: by and large, local law enforcement around the South was either in cahoots with the KKK or helpless to combat the outlaws. Nothing short of federal intervention could crush the KKK.

With President Grant's full support, Congress stepped in with "force acts," legislation to enforce rights guaranteed in the Fourteenth and Fifteenth Amendments. Among other things, the new laws made it a crime, punishable by fines and imprisonment, to interfere with a person's right to vote and authorized the president to use troops to uphold the new laws.

The strongest measure was the "Ku Klux Klan Act" (April 1871). It gave the federal government the power to punish the kinds of crimes the KKK and other terrorist groups engaged in. Conspiracies to violate people's rights could essentially be treated as acts of rebellion against the federal government. In crushing a rebellion, the president could suspend the writ of *habeas corpus* (Latin for "you shall have the body"), which made it illegal to imprison people without charging them with a crime in a court of law. Congress also formed another joint committee to investigate Southern violence.

President Grant hoped the threat of martial law would motivate white Southerners to rein in the terrorists in their midst. He was not hankering to use absolute power, but reports of KKK rampages in South Carolina's Piedmont region and Governor Robert Scott's request for help compelled him to do so in mid-October 1871. Grant proclaimed nine South Carolina counties in a state of rebellion.

"The most stupendous lie." That's what a resident of Rock Hill, York County, South Carolina, said of Grant's proclamation. "There is no rebellion; there is no hostility to the United States government," the man insisted in a letter to former Maryland senator Reverdy Johnson. The South Carolinian claimed that soldiers were galloping around "arresting citizens by the wholesale, tearing them from their homes in the night time, terrifying women and children, hurrying the prisoners off to jail and cramming them into dungeons and filthy cells." The man's brother had been among those jailed.

The letter, with the man's name omitted, appeared in a November 1871 issue of Washington Territory's *Walla Walla Statesman,* which did not have a lot of love for the Hero of Appomattox. The newspaper claimed that the arrests in South Carolina were a harbinger of things to come. Grant would soon sic troops on other parts of the South, readers were told, because Southern Republicans urged him "daily to take these violent steps" so they could hold on to power.

President Grant was not eager to send more troops *anywhere.* The army

"THE BURNING OF CHICAGO," from James McCabe's 1875 book ***The Centennial History of the United States***. *More than three hundred people died in the Great Chicago Fire. About a hundred thousand people were rendered homeless. Property damage and destruction totaled over $200 million.*

could not police the entire nation! Shortly before he declared martial law in some of South Carolina, a fire that started on Patrick and Catherine O'Leary's farm in the Windy City became the Great Chicago Fire. Looting kicked up the chaos. Grant sent General Sheridan to the rescue. The general pulled in ten companies of troops from various forts for relief-giving and peacekeeping duties.

Of course, no one took issue with the use of troops in Chicago's calamity, but the use of the military to protect the rights—and lives—of blacks and white Republicans in the South was coming increasingly under fire outside the South. The Ku Klux Klan Act had not received unanimous support among Republicans in Congress. During House debates on the bill, Illinois representative John Farnsworth worried that Congress was overdoing it: giving the federal government too much power and trampling states' rights. "Six years have elapsed since the war closed," said Farnsworth. "We have reconstructed, and reconstructed, and we are asked to reconstruct again by clothing the President with power to use the Army and the Navy of the United States, or any other means which he may deem proper. . . . [A]nd I fear we are governing the South too much." By the end of 1871, more Republicans agreed with Farnsworth.

But the power Congress had given Grant had made a difference. About two thousand Klansmen were jailed; several hundred faced trial. Many got off scot-free because witnesses refused to testify against them out of sympathy or fear. In other cases, friends and kin provided bogus alibis. Still, martial law had caused the KKK to lie low. But by then the terrorism had had the intended effect.

"The Ku-Klux labors have proved successful [in Alabama]," reported an article in a mid-October 1872 issue of *Harper's Weekly*. KKK activity in Alabama included the murder of several pro–Republican Party ministers— one shot in his pulpit.

Alabama was not unique. The *Harper's Weekly* article made that clear. The KKK had "terrified and subdued Louisiana, it swept over Texas; mounted and disguised ruffians rode through Mississippi in 1871, breaking up the colored

*From the October 19, 1872, issue of **Harper's Weekly**. The artist supposed that a pro–Democratic Party Southern newspaper would caption this scene "ONE VOTE LESS."*

schools, and driving away preachers, and teachers; they covered Western Tennessee; they murdered, whipped, tormented in North Carolina." In Georgia, "whole counties of colored voters are disfranchised by the terrors."

The congressional committee investigating the terrorism had issued a report several thousand pages long. It contained killings like the ones *Harper's Weekly* reported and testimony about beatings like the one Georgia legislator Abram Colby endured. South Carolina representative Robert Elliott testified that the KKK had killed about six hundred Republicans in his state. Florida's secretary of state, Jonathan Gibbs, reported 153 murders in Jackson County alone. Betsey Westbrook of Demopolis, Alabama, recounted the night Klansmen broke into her home and shot her husband dead in front of her. When asked "What were they mad at your husband about?" she replied, "He just would hold up his head and say he was a strong Radical."

*Ohio-born Victoria Claflin Woodhull. She and her sister, Tennessee Claflin, were faith healers and fortune-tellers for a time. After they moved to New York City in the late 1860s and became friends with tycoon Cornelius Vanderbilt, they shifted into financial wizardry. In 1870, with their stock profits and funds from Vanderbilt, the sisters opened the first female-owned brokerage firm. Their Wall Street offices also housed their newspaper, **Woodhull & Claflin Weekly**. When Woodhull ran for president on the Equal Rights Party ticket in 1872, she ran on a platform that included women's suffrage, civil rights for blacks, and abolition of the death penalty. Her party had wanted Fred Douglass to be her running mate, but he wanted to campaign for Grant.*

Economic terrorism went hand in hand with violence. Some white Southerners, members of the KKK and not, refused to sell or rent land or homes to Republicans and boycotted Republican-owned businesses. Where whites controlled the school system, some sought to sabotage black futures by underfunding black schools (most attempts at integrating public schools failed). As more Republicans left the South or quit politics, more Democrats came into power. But Republicans held on to the White House.

In the 1872 elections, Ulysses S. Grant beat out his top competition, Horace Greeley, chief of the *New York Tribune*. Greeley had been for the abolition of slavery and for impeaching Andy Johnson, but he thought Congressional Reconstruction too severe. He left the Republican Party for the spin-off Liberal Republican Party. It was big on stamping out corruption in government and supported a milder policy on the South. Unable to field a candidate with huge appeal, the Democratic Party had gotten behind Greeley. Among the other losers, one made history: the Equal Rights Party's candidate,

Pinckney Benton Stewart Pinchback, the first black to serve, albeit briefly, as governor of a state, and the last until L. Douglas Wilder was elected governor of Virginia in 1989. Georgia-born Pinchback, the son of a free woman and a white planter, spent much of his youth in Cincinnati, Ohio. As a young man, he worked as a steward aboard steamboats that traveled the Mississippi River. During the war, Pinchback settled in New Orleans and served in the Union Army.

Victoria Woodhull, the first woman in America to run for president.

The year ended with another first for blacks. When Louisiana's (and America's) first black lieutenant governor, Oscar Dunn, had died, P.B.S. Pinchback, the state senate's president *pro tem*, had replaced him. Then, when Governor Henry Warmoth was impeached for alleged corruption and removed from office, Pinchback, whose own integrity was not above reproach, became the nation's first black governor— but only for a few weeks, until the recently elected governor, Republican William Kellogg, took office, following hotly contested elections. The Democrats claimed that their slate of candidates had really been the victors. The state militia, loyal to the Democratic Party, was poised to oust Kellogg and company, but the Republicans had President Grant's backing. He authorized federal troops to step in. Louisiana was a time bomb. Seven years after the Civil War ended—still no peace.

The Woman's Journal.

VOL. IV. BOSTON, CHICAGO AND ST. LOUIS, SATURDAY, JANUARY 25, 1873. NO. 4.

THE WOMAN'S JOURNAL.
— AND —
THE WOMAN'S ADVOCATE,
CONSOLIDATED AUGUST 13, 1870.
A Weekly Newspaper, published every Saturday, in Boston and Chicago, devoted to the interests of Woman, to her educational, industrial, legal and political Equality, and especially to her right of Suffrage.

JULIA WARD HOWE.................
LUCY STONE.......................
HENRY B. BLACKWELL............. EDITORS.
T. W. HIGGINSON.................
MARY A. LIVERMORE, CORRESPONDING EDITOR.

MISS INGELOW'S QUESTION.

In a certain New England town, I lived opposite the house of a thriving mechanic. His wife, a young and pretty woman, soon attracted the attention of my household by the grace and dignity of her bearing, and the peculiar tastefulness of her own and her little boy's costume. On farther acquaintance, we found that she did every atom of her house-work, washing and all; that she cut and made every

far. Women will never compete equally with men, until they are willing, like men, to do any honest work without sense of degradation. This is one point where enfranchisement will help them. So long as a man bears in his hand the ballot, that symbol of substantial equality, his self-respect is not easily impaired by the humblest position—"A man's a man for a' that," he knows, before the law. But a woman, not having this, has only the usages

ished till 1834, and practically never to the present hour; for who is more enslaved than tens of thousands in England, driven daily to unremunerative toil under the lash of a necessity sharper, more stinging, and hardly less degrading than the snap of whip-cord? Verily, if, as publicists and jurists have dreamed, society is intended to be an association of interests to protect the weak against the strong, then is society, as says Montesquieu, "a most magnificent

CONCERNING WOMEN.

Two of the pension agencies of this country are managed by women.

Gen. Schenck's youngest daughter is to marry an English nobleman.

Mme. de Perinot has left 20,000 francs to the French Academy to found a prize for astronomical researches.

*Lucy Stone and Julia Ward Howe launched **The Woman's Journal** in January 1870, on the second anniversary of Susan Anthony's newspaper, **The Revolution**. Howe had published an antislavery newspaper with her husband, Samuel, but was best known for the poem that became the Union's beloved marching song, "The Battle Hymn of the Republic." The other two editors listed above had also been abolitionists. Stone's husband, Henry Blackwell, was the brother of Drs. Elizabeth and Emily Blackwell. Colonel Thomas Wentworth Higginson had served with the first black regiment raised in South Carolina.*

While blacks fought for their civil rights, women's rights activists kept crusading for women's suffrage. "An important question is likely soon to be settled by the approaching trial of Susan B. Anthony," stated the *Woman's Journal* on January 25, 1873. Anthony had been indicted for voting.

In the November 1872 elections, Anthony had convinced befuddled voting officials in Rochester, New York, that the Fourteenth Amendment entitled her to vote. Her argument (with a threat to sue them) claimed that because she met the requirements for "citizen" (in her case, born in the United States), she was entitled to citizens' "privileges"—topmost, the right to vote. Granted, the Fourteenth Amendment linked a state's representation in Congress to male suffrage, but it did not explicitly say that only men could vote. Getting arrested, then indicted—it had played out just as Anthony had hoped. She wanted a women's suffrage court case. The *Woman's Journal* applauded her scheme.

The same issue of the newspaper had articles urging women to do less corset wearing and more exercising and carried items on successes and setbacks for

*After Susan Anthony was found guilty, she refused to pay the fine and court costs as ordered. The judge let it go, thus denying her another arrest and more publicity. This article is from the July 5, 1873, issue of **Harper's Weekly**.*

others were driven out, and the building was fired.

Mr. KENNEDY, who was making a tour of inspection to ascertain the feeling among the populace, came upon the scene of the trouble while the uproar was at its height. Being a man of dauntless courage, he alighted from his carriage, and advanced toward the infuriated mob. He was at once recognized. With a brutal yell the crowd rushed upon him, bore him to the ground, and beat and trod upon him until he became insensible. Believing they had killed him, the brutal mob flung his body into a gutter and fled. He was soon afterward picked up by some friends, and conveyed to Police Head-quarters, where his wounds were dressed. He was found to be terribly bruised, but, fortunately, no bones were broken.

On his partial recovery from the effects of this cowardly assault, Mr. KENNEDY resumed active command of the force, and remained the executive head until 1870, when, by the passage of the charter, the system was changed from the Metropolitan to the Municipal Police Force, and he was legislated out of office after an honorable service of eleven years. Mr. KENNEDY resigned, and Captain JOURDAN was appointed to fill the position.

By the death of Mr. KENNEDY New York loses a well-tried and faithful servant, and the Republican party a member to whose public record it can point with unqualified approval. He made our police force what it is. His devotion to the public service during a most trying and critical period was exemplary and unswerving. His power of organization and exceptional faculty of command brought the city through the terrible strain of July, 1863; and it was his spirit which animated the police during the critical ordeal of July 12, 1871.

At the time of his death Mr. KENNEDY held the position of Collector of Assessments for this city.

SUSAN B. ANTHONY'S VOTE.

MISS SUSAN B. ANTHONY, the redoubtable champion and exponent of the political rights of women, has at length come to grief at the hands of the law. Not satisfied with promulgating her "peculiar" views from the platform and through the press, she determined to make a test of the matter at the ballot-box, and the

SUSAN B. ANTHONY.

result must be discouraging in the extreme. In the last November election, it will be remembered, Miss ANTHONY voted, in the city of Rochester, New York, the Congressional, State, and Assembly tickets. This she did in the belief that the right of suffrage was conveyed to her sex under the Fourteenth Amendment of the Constitution of the United States, which defines citizens as "*all persons* born or naturalized in the United States, and subject to the jurisdiction thereof." The authorities, however, took quite a different view of the matter, and Miss ANTHONY was arrested and indicted for illegal voting.

The trial of the case was held on the 17th June, in the Circuit Court of the United States sitting at Canandaigua, Judge HUNT presiding. Mr. RICHARD CROWLEY, the District Attorney, conducted the prosecution, and Judge HENRY R. SELDEN and Mr. JOHN VAN VOORHIS appeared for the defense. The judge directed the jury to find the defendant "guilty," and a fine of $100 and costs was imposed. The inspectors who received the vote were also convicted, and fined $25 each, with costs.

the women's movement—"CALL FOR A WOMAN SUFFRAGE CONVENTION IN MAINE," "WOMAN'S RIGHTS RIDICULED" (about a play mocking feminists), "ARRAIGNED, TRIED, CONVICTED" (thoughts on Anna Dickinson's recent lecture in Boston on women in the work world), and "THE CAUSE IN OHIO" (on apathy and anti–women's suffrage sentiments among women there). The newspaper offered tidbits on women of distinction in its "Concerning

Women" column. Evangelist Amanda Smith had recently visited Cincinnati, where "crowded houses waited upon her ministry." The writer Grace Greenwood had purchased land in Manitou, Colorado, "near the soda springs," with plans to build a house there. Elizabeth Colt, widow of firearms titan Samuel Colt, was making eight hundred thousand dollars a year in gun sales. "She supplies the New York markets liberally, as is proved by the frequent murders that are perpetrated with her pistol," the column said.

Colt revolvers and other guns were in liberal use around the nation by bank and train robbers, by ranchers against cattle rustlers, by marks against card sharks, by soldiers and western homesteaders against Native Americans, and vice versa. Guns were also in play in black-white conflicts, like the one that erupted in April 1873 in Louisiana in a newly created town, in a newly created parish, named after the vice president and the president. The violence was rooted in the bitterly disputed state elections of 1872.

After the radical Louisiana governor William Kellogg was firmly in place, he made some changes to shore up his power. In Grant Parish, where the black-white ratio was about fifty-fifty (population about forty-five hundred), Kellogg replaced the opposition party's sheriff and judge with Radical Republicans. Anticipating trouble, black men in Colfax, the parish seat, turned the courthouse into a fortress. About two hundred members of an emerging terror group, the White League, amassed at the courthouse at the behest of the ousted sheriff. The black men held their ground. The White Leaguers had plenty of ammunition, and no compunction about setting the building on fire. When the smoke cleared, two whites were dead. Some sources put the black death count at fifty. Others say it climbed to around three hundred. Most of the black men had been shot after they had laid down their arms and exited the courthouse, white flag and all.

Colfax was one of the relatively rare times that blacks did anything like go on the offensive. Some argue that this did not occur more often because one consequence of eighty thousand days of slavery in America was that blacks were

AME evangelist Amanda Berry Smith, whose "rich contralto voice with which she would break into song when inspired, made her a person not easily forgotten," according to a contemporary. Smith was one of five children born into slavery (Maryland). By 1840, her father had liberated his children and his wife with the almighty dollar after purchasing his own liberty. A decade later, the family was living in York, Pennsylvania. Their home was an Underground Railroad station.

*This engraving, captioned "THE LOUISIANA MURDERS—GATHERING THE DEAD AND WOUNDED," ran in **Harper's Weekly** a few weeks after the Colfax massacre in its May 10, 1873, issue.*

scared to the bone of whites. Others think not. The reluctance to use violence and rough justice "extended up and down the Republican hierarchy, and was not confined to one race," contends historian Eric Foner. "Perhaps the problem was that Republicans, black and white, took democratic processes more seriously than their opponents. . . . [N]o Republicans rode at night to murder their political foes, nor did armed bands seek to drive Democrats from the polls." Not that the thought never occurred to them. "We could burn their churches and school-houses, but we don't want to break the law or harm anybody," said a black man in Georgia. "All we want is to live under the law."

Lack of firepower was also a factor, especially down South. Even where blacks outnumbered whites, they were outgunned. If anything, most blacks had shotguns, potentially lethal, yes, but, as Foner points out, "much inferior to the 'first-class weapons' like Winchester rifles and six-shooters" in the hands of white terrorists in a region where "virtually every white male had been trained to bear arms." The majority of black men in the South had no such training. At war's end, many black soldiers who were in the South moved north or west after they mustered out. Almost all blacks in the postwar army were in the Far West, for two reasons: to placate white Southerners who resented black soldiers in their midst and to protect national interests, especially the railroads, those up and running and under construction.

After the 1869 wedding of the rails at Promontory Point, railroad building zoomed. Hordes of individuals and institutions bought up railroad stock like crazy. But railroad building went too fast. In late 1873, the railroad boom went bust—too much railroad, not enough profit. The value of railroad stocks plummeted as investors rushed to sell theirs. To stop the sell-off, the New York Stock Exchange closed on September 20, 1873. When it reopened ten days later, the Washington, D.C., newspaper *Daily Critic* told readers, under the header "The Financial Flurry," that it had "every reason to believe that the great panic has passed away." The newspaper reported that the "President and Secretary of the Treasury now believe that the prospects are bright, and that all danger is past." In its "Social Gossip" column, the newspaper told readers that white sealskin would be de rigueur when it came to fur fashions, the "$10 suit at Saks & Co.'s" was the "best in the city for the money," and "ladies' hats this season consist chiefly of two bows of ribbon and a stiff feather." The *Daily Critic* may have been right about fashion, but it was wrong about the financial "flurry."

It was a blizzard. The Panic of 1873 spiraled into a dogged economic depression. Scores of banks heavily invested in railroad stocks failed. Not until after the Great Depression of the 1930s did the federal government create the Federal Deposit Insurance Corporation (FDIC). It guarantees that if a bank in

"SCENE IN THE NEW YORK STOCK EXCHANGE DURING THE PANIC OF 1873," from James McCabe's 1875 book **The Centennial History of the United States**. *The panic was set off by the collapse of the nation's leading bank, Jay Cooke and Company. It was the underwriter for the Northern Pacific Railroad, which had received a land grant of over forty million acres in Dakota and Montana territories. Cooke had raised millions of dollars for the railroad in bonds. When his bank failed, investors lost about $100 million.*

*This ad for what is known as the "Freedman's Bank" ran in the issue of the **Daily Critic** that reported on the "financial flurry." The bank was created by an act of Congress (March 1865) to give black people a respectful place to work on their financial freedom. Headquartered in D.C. (1507 Pennsylvania Avenue), it had close to forty branches in over a dozen states (mostly in the South). By the early 1870s, the bank had around a hundred thousand customers (individuals along with churches and other institutions) and deposits totaling nearly $60 million.*

FREEDMAN'S SAVINGS AND TRUST COMPANY.—This institution, which has twice lately given evidence of its solidity, offers extraordinary inducements to depositors. As will be seen by their advertisement, all profits are divided among depositors, as interest, not exceeding seven per cent. per annum; and, further, interest is allowed on all deposits from the first of the month, in sums of one dollar and upwards. These advantages, together with the proved safety of the institution, should be thought of by those who desire to deposit their earnings and have them accumulate.

its program fails, the government will give people at least some of the money they had on deposit (initially up to $2,500; today, up to $100,000 per account). Before the FDIC, when a bank declared itself broke, its customers' money—gone. So in the Panic of 1873, with money gone, some people sold their jewels and other valuables; others tightened their belts. With money gone, mortgages went unpaid and banks foreclosed on homes and farms. With money gone, businesses cut wages and laid off workers. Some eighteen thousand businesses—factories, mills, shops—went belly up by 1875. The population of the homeless—"tramps"—soared.

*On January 13, 1874, a deep-freeze day in New York City, over seven thousand people turned out for a rally in Lower Manhattan's Tompkins Square. A sizeable contingent belonged to the New York chapter of the International Workingmen's Association. The people planned to march on City Hall to compel the city to initiate a public assistance program for the unemployed. Police compelled the people to beat it by charging into the crowd, billy clubs at the ready. "It was the most glorious sight I ever saw," proclaimed Police Commissioner Abram Duryee, a former Union Army general. **Frank Leslie's Illustrated Newspaper** apparently agreed with Duryee. When this engraving appeared in its January 31, 1874, issue, it was captioned "THE RED FLAG IN NEW YORK—RIOTOUS COMMUNIST WORKINGMEN DRIVEN FROM TOMPKINS SQUARE BY THE MOUNTED POLICE."*

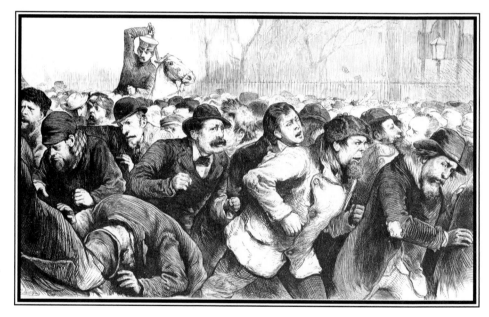

From an 1874 lithograph titled "THE SHACKLE BROKEN—BY THE GENIUS OF FREEDOM," featuring South Carolina representative Robert Brown Elliott speaking for a civil rights bill in the House on January 6, 1874. Some early accounts of Elliott's life said that he was born in Boston to parents who had been forever free. Others, that he was the son of South Carolinians who had escaped from slavery. Today many scholars believe that he was born in Liverpool, England. If true, as his biographer Peggy Lamson has written, Elliott is "the only British subject ever to be a member of the House of Representatives of the United States of America."

The Republican Party's interest in the plight of blacks had declined even more by early 1874, but there were still some Republicans with racial justice very much on their minds. One of them was South Carolina representative

Robert Elliott. He took to the floor of the House in early January 1874 to urge passage of another civil rights bill. This one outlawed discrimination in hotels, trains, and other places of public accommodation. It also called for public school desegregation. Outlawing segregated schools would be an equalizer, thwarting the widespread policy of scrimping on schools for black children. Some people also thought that if black and white children learned together, they would learn to respect each other.

In his speech, Robert Elliott said in so many words that it was a sin and a shame that anyone should have to "rise in the presence of an American Congress to advocate a bill which simply asserts equal rights and equal public privileges for all classes of American citizens."

The civil rights bill's "father" was Senator Charles "Stick" Sumner. He had introduced it in 1870, and time and again he couldn't get enough votes for it to pass. Hoping that the spirit of fair play would prevail, in 1872 Sumner attached it to an amnesty bill restoring to all but a few ex-Confederates the right to hold public office that was taken away in the Fourteenth Amendment. "There is beauty in art, in literature, in science, and in every triumph of intelligence . . . but there is a higher beauty still," he said in a Senate speech. "There is true grandeur in an example of justice, making the rights of all the same as our own, and beating down prejudice, like Satan, under our feet." The majority of Republicans cared more about mollifying ex-Confederates than supporting the civil rights of blacks. The amnesty bill passed, stripped of Sumner's equal rights initiative.

Massachusetts senator Charles Sumner. He became all the more a hero to fellow abolitionists in spring 1856, after South Carolina representative Preston Brooks gave him a beating with a metal-tipped walking cane in the Senate chamber. Sumner had recently delivered an impassioned speech against Kansas being admitted into the Union as a slave state, in the process insulting Brooks's relative Senator Andrew Butler (Democrat–South Carolina). Sumner's injuries were so severe that he did not return to the Senate for about three years.

"The constitution of a free government ought always to be construed in favor of human rights," Robert Elliott insisted in his 1874 speech on Sumner's bill. Elliott stressed that the Thirteenth, Fourteenth, and Fifteenth Amendments "invest Congress with the power to protect the citizen in his civil and political rights." *Use that power!* he urged.

There were six other black members of the House then: James

"THE FIRST COLORED SENATOR AND REPRESENTATIVES"
In the 41st and 42nd Congress of the United States
(back row, left to right) Rep. Robert DeLarge (SC), Rep. Jefferson Long (GA); (front row, left to right) Sen. Hiram Revels (MS), Rep. Benjamin Turner (AL), Rep. Josiah Walls (FL), Rep. Joseph Rainey (SC), Rep. Robert Elliott (SC)

Black congressmen were not in lockstep on all matters. Jefferson Franklin Long, who had headed up the branch of the Union League in Macon, Georgia, was vehemently opposed to the act that lifted the Fourteenth Amendment's ban on certain ex-Confederates holding public office. Those men were "the very men who have committed these Ku Klux outrages," he charged. Joseph Hayne Rainey, however, favored amnesty. There were class tensions as well. Robert Carlos DeLarge, who traveled in elitist mulatto circles, was considered refined. Benjamin Sterling Turner, who had amassed a small fortune from his enterprises (hotel and livery stable), irked some of his colleagues because he was a little rough around the edges. Surely, the people who benefited from his largesse, like the children who attended the Alabama school he financed, didn't care about his manners.

Rapier (Alabama); Josiah Walls (Florida); John Lynch (Mississippi); and Joseph Rainey, Richard Cain, and Alonzo Ransier (all from South Carolina). In pressing for the bill's passage, several recounted humiliations they had endured: denial of service in a restaurant, denial of a seat in a first-class train coach. If that could happen to congressmen, how much worse for everyday black folks, like Sarah Thompson, a schoolteacher in Memphis, Tennessee. In 1872, Thompson had sent Charles Sumner a letter in which she recounted what she and her four children (the oldest was eleven) suffered during a journey from Cincinnati, Ohio, to Memphis.

It was wintertime. During a layover in Louisville, Kentucky, Thompson and her children had not been permitted inside the train station's waiting room. "Why is this, Ma?" one of her freezing, sleet-whipped children asked as the family paced back and forth in front of the depot to work off some of the cold. "What have we done? Why can't we go in there and warm up just like the others?" When the train arrived, Thompson and her children were forced to ride in the smoking car, "to sit and inhale fumes of tobacco rising from the cigars and pipes . . . also, to hear all manner of obscene and profane language." At the end of her letter, the schoolteacher wrote, "I sincerely hope your bill may pass." Two years later, despite all efforts—despite the fact that, according to the *Congressional Record*, Robert Elliott's speech received "great applause"—the civil rights bill failed to pass, at a time when Republicans still had a majority in the House (more than two to one), as they did in the Senate. Several weeks later, in March, Charles Sumner died. As he ebbed, George Downing and Fred Douglass were among those by his side.

At the time, Douglass was at the helm of the Freedman's Bank, a dying institution. Almost all its white board members had jumped ship when Douglass was tapped to captain it. Douglass knew nothing about banking, nor that the bank was a wreck. Instead of staying with the safe government securities its original charter prescribed, the directors had gotten Congress to permit the bank to invest in potentially high-profit—and thus high-risk—stocks, such as railroad stocks. When Douglass realized the bank was sinking, he pumped some of his own money into it. It was too little, too late. The bank went under in June 1874. Millions of dollars that blacks had deposited—for many, nickels and dimes at a time—gone.

When the Freedman's Bank collapsed, Louisiana, Florida, Mississippi, and South Carolina were the only ex-CSA states that did not have Democratic governors and Democrat-controlled legislatures. Whites in those states who had pledged to wrest control from Republicans called themselves "Redeemers."

Coushatta, Louisiana, was one place Redeemers worked their malice. In August 1874, in the run-up to local and state elections, a White League posse rounded up and shot dead about two dozen Republicans, some black, some white, some officeholders. The victims included the brother and brothers-in-law of Vermont-born Marshall Twitchell, former commander of a black regiment and Freedmen's Bureau agent turned successful planter and Louisiana state senator. Twitchell wasn't in Coushatta when his kin and the other men were killed. Some time later, back in Coushatta, an assassination attempt resulted in the amputation of his arms.

A few months after the Coushatta massacre, in Vicksburg, Mississippi, whites demanded the ouster of Warren County's black sheriff, Peter Crosby. When people came to Crosby's defense, blacks and whites shed blood in the streets. Members of a terror group, the White Man's Party, went on a shooting and whipping spree. President Grant sent troops to stop the "Vicksburg troubles." Shortly thereafter, trouble kicked up again in Louisiana, this time in New Orleans.

Several members of the White League declared themselves the true winners in the 1874 elections. On January 4, 1875, they stormed the Louisiana statehouse to oust Republicans. Grant directed troops to reinstate the Republicans. He sent the general most white Louisianans loved to hate, Phil Sheridan. Declare the White Leaguers "banditti" and shoot them—that's what General Sheridan proposed. Grant did not allow it, but he was still castigated in newspapers and around dinner tables, North and South, for using federal force. *Tyrant!* people hissed.

Grant was incensed over the violence in the South—and the flak he was getting for trying to stop it. This was abundantly clear in his message to the Senate on January 13, in response to its request that he explain himself.

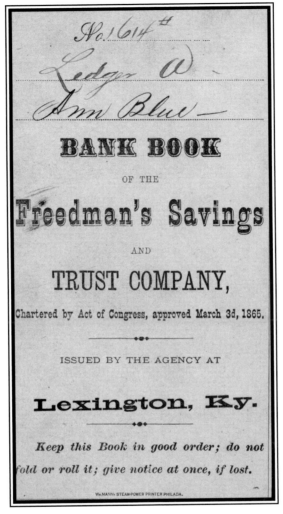

Ann Blue opened her Freedman's Bank account with $50 in 1873. When the bank collapsed, she had $61.20 on deposit. The government had the bank's assets sold. The proceeds were earmarked for its roughly sixty thousand customers. They had to request their money by mailing in their bank books to an office in D.C. Between 1875 and 1883, about half of the depositors received about 62 percent of the money they were owed. Ann Blue was among them.

"Fierce denunciations ring through the country about office-holding and election matters in Louisiana, while every one of the Colfax miscreants goes unwhipped of justice, and no way can be found in this boasted land of civilization and Christianity to punish the perpetrators of this bloody and monstrous crime." Grant also brought up the victims of Coushatta: "No one has been punished." What's more, Louisiana's pro–Democratic Party newspapers "denounced" all attempts to bring the culprits to justice and "boldly justified the crime." Colfax and Coushatta were not isolated incidents, he reminded the Senate. "A great number of such murders have been committed and no one has been punished."

The only arrow Republicans had in their quiver was Sumner's civil rights bill. It finally passed on March 1, 1875. By then the section on school desegregation had been excised from what is known as the Civil Rights Act of 1875. Violation of the law carried a penalty of a five-hundred-to-one-thousand-dollar fine or incarceration for thirty days to a year. But would the law be enforced? In the current climate, if a train conductor forced a black person to ride in a filthy smoking car or if a restaurant refused to serve a black couple, the criminals would likely go "unwhipped of justice."

A few days after the civil rights bill passed, Andy Johnson took his seat in the U.S. Senate, having finally won a congressional race. He wasn't in office for long. Following a stroke, he died in late July 1875. He was buried in Greeneville, Tennessee. As requested, his body was wrapped in an American flag and a copy of the Constitution was placed beneath his head. Johnson had made history as the first U.S. senator who was a former president; and he had earned the everlasting enmity of legions of Americans who believed in racial justice.

As for President Grant, he faced another crisis when Mississippi Redeemers unleashed a reign of terror just before the local and state elections of 1875. And Redeemers had their way. For example, in Yazoo

Governor Adelbert Ames, son-in-law of Ben "The Beast" Butler. Ames, born in Maine, was a West Point graduate. He received the Congressional Medal of Honor for valor in the 1861 Battle of Bull Run.

County, about 75 percent black, of the roughly four thousand votes cast, only seven were Republican. Mississippi's governor, Adelbert Ames, had pleaded with Grant to send troops. His request was denied. Grant and his party were still fending off criticisms of his earlier use of troops in the South and the charge of *Tyrant!* With a presidential election coming up, the Republican Party didn't want to give white voters more cause for complaint, even if it meant outrages and slaughter for Mississippians so long so loyal to that party.

The presidency had no term limits then, but Grant would not run again. He was sick of politics, and the Republican Party had soured on the Hero of Appomattox. The use of troops in the South wasn't the only issue. Grant's administrations had been peppered with scandals. One of the earliest broke in 1872: a pack of politicians were accused of taking bribes from the Union Pacific Railroad for not delving into the company's scheme by which it scammed the government of over $20 million (the Crédit Mobilier scandal). The accused bribe takers included Schuyler "The Smiler" Colfax. That's why he was dumped as Grant's running mate in 1872 and replaced with Henry Wilson. That scandal was part of the inspiration for Mark Twain's 1873 novel, *The Gilded Age*. The term came to apply to late-nineteenth-century America as an era of corruption, capitalism, and consumerism run amok ("gilded" in the sense of a golden covering for something rather worthless).

So the new year brought a fresh Republican presidential candidate. And not only that: 1876 was also the year of America's grandest celebration of herself the world had yet seen.

In looking back on Grant's time as president, this cartoon from the February 4, 1880, issue of the humor magazine **Puck** makes the point that had Grant run for a third term, he would have had to be quite the political acrobat. Some of the people caught up in scandals are pictured here. They include Grant's private secretary, General Orville Babcock (bottom right, holding a ring). Babcock was one of about two hundred men indicted in 1875 as part of the "Whiskey Ring": distilleries in St. Louis, Chicago, and other Midwestern cities bribed treasury agents to look the other way as they cooked the books, defrauding the government of about $3 million in taxes. Secretary of the Navy George Robeson (center, both hands on the bar) reportedly accrued $300,000 in bribes from defense contractors. Robeson's legs are wrapped around Attorney General George Williams, who used government money to pay off personal bills he and his lavish-lifestyle-loving wife ran up.

"THE PROMISES IN YOUR CONSTITUTION"

MEMORIAL HALL

MACHINERY HALL

WOMEN'S PAVILION

*"THE CENTENNIAL—BALLOON VIEW OF THE GROUNDS," a supplement to the September 30, 1876, issue of **Harper's Weekly**. The exposition's official name was the International Exhibition of Arts, Manufactures, and Products of the Soil and Mine. More than thirty nations exhibited at America's second world's fair. Feminists were irritated by the Women's Pavilion because (1) it was an afterthought and (2) it focused on sewing and other domestic arts, reinforcing the prevailing notion that a woman's place is in the home. Representations of blacks at the Centennial were stereotypical (ditto for Native Americans), but two black artists made a mark. Edward Mitchell Bannister's landscape **Under the Oaks** won the first-place award for oil paintings. Edmonia Lewis's huge sculpture **The Death of Cleopatra** was noticed (if not universally liked). Both were on display in Memorial Hall.*

The event had been in the planning for several years. An army of carpenters, masons, and other artisans and laborers had built about two hundred buildings and beautified the grounds of Fairmount Park in the City of Brotherly Love, the nation's first capital. The occasion was America's celebration of the hundredth anniversary of the Declaration of Independence: its break from Great Britain, its promise to be a land of liberty.

The six-month Centennial Exposition opened on May 10, 1876. Most of America (population upwards of forty million) could not enjoy it in person. The unemployment rate was 14 percent. Among the employed, the average worker made about a dollar a day; it cost fifty cents to get into the Centennial. So not a lot of people could afford the entrance fee, let alone the cost of transportation and lodgings if they lived far from Philadelphia.

Those who had the price of the ticket browsed the wares of such individual companies as Pennsylvania File Works. They surveyed the prides of states, like the Kansas display, with its yards of jars of buckwheat, barley, broomcorn, millet, sorghum, flax, timothy, and other grains. "The Leviathan Incubator," an ostrich egg hatchery from South Africa, was among the wonders of other nations. With so many people enthralled by the technological innovations of the second Industrial Revolution, Machinery Hall was perpetually popular. George Corliss's seven-hundred-ton steam engine and Scottish émigré Aleck Bell's telephone were among its main attractions.

The centerpiece of the Centennial was, of course, July 4. Independence Day ceremonies at Independence Hall included a reading of the original Declaration of Independence, frail and faded, by Richard Henry Lee, whose grandfather and great-uncle had been among its fifty-six signers. Susan Anthony and a small corps of suffragists were in the audience. When Lee finished his reading, Anthony strode up to the podium with a scroll inscribed with a Declaration of Rights for Women. She firmly placed it into the hands of the man presiding over the ceremonies. Weeks earlier, she and Elizabeth Cady Stanton had asked to present their declaration as part of the ceremonies. "No," they were told.

After her act of defiance, Anthony and company left the ceremonies, handing out copies of their declaration as they did. In a nearby bandstand, Anthony read it aloud. The document ended with: "We ask justice, we ask equality, we ask that all civil and political rights that belong to the citizens of the United States be guaranteed to our daughters forever."

Several hundred miles away in Hamburg, South Carolina, a black militia's Independence Day parade brought two white men in a buggy to a halt. The black men made a part in their ranks through which the buggy could pass, but not before an exchange of ugly words. Area whites would not leave it alone. They wanted the black militia to turn over their weapons. When the black men refused to disarm, unlike Susan Anthony, they paid dearly for their defiance. After the initial shoot-out, droves of whites from across the Savannah

During the Hamburg massacre, whites repeatedly proclaimed, "This is the beginning of the redemption of South Carolina," according to Dock Adams, the leader of the town's militia. This image is a detail from an engraving in the August 12, 1876, issue of **Harper's Weekly**. *Artist Thomas Nast projects what Redeemers often meant by "reform."*

River in Augusta, Georgia, poured into Hamburg and added to the litany of Reconstruction-era massacres.

Yet another massacre sprang from George Armstrong Custer's decision to lead the 7th Cavalrymen in an attack on a Native American encampment near the Little Bighorn River on June 25, 1876. News of "Custer's Last Stand," his death, and that of the roughly two hundred soldiers under his direct command did not reach most Americans until around the Fourth of July. When it did, there arose a frenzy for total war against Native Americans who said no to the reservation.

Along with reports on the stepped-up war against Native Americans and such events as statehood for Colorado (August) and the Jesse James–Bob

A scene from the Battle of Little Bighorn (Custer, far left), as imagined by Frederic Remington. Custer's attack was part of a campaign to remove Native Americans from Montana Territory's Black Hills after the discovery of gold in the area. The Native American forces fighting expulsion from their land were led by Lakota chief Tatanka-Iyotanka (Sitting Bull) and Tashunca-Uitco (Crazy Horse). Montana Territory was organized in 1864 out of Idaho Territory, which had been organized in 1863 out of parts of Washington and Dakota territories.

Younger gang's foiled bank robbery in Northfield, Minnesota (early September), newspapers continued to keep people abreast of the Centennial. A September 1876 issue of *Harper's Weekly* reported on China's pavilion, with its fetching display of "lacquered ware and rich carvings" and "rich silks of delicate shades of color." Also in that issue was a letter from a Texan slamming courts as "the most infamous engines of persecution and oppression" of blacks.

The U.S. Supreme Court had neutered the amendments to the Constitution intended to empower blacks and protect their civil rights along with those of white Republicans in the South. The court did this in 1873, when it ruled on the "Slaughterhouse Cases," which turned on a piece of pro–Big Business legislation in the Pelican State. Louisiana lawmakers had allowed a corporation to have a virtual monopoly on New Orleans's butchering business. Because this action would put many local mom-and-pop meat markets out of business, a group of white butchers sued the state to overturn the law. Counsel for the butchers argued that this restriction on their liberty violated the due-process clause of the Fourteenth Amendment ("nor shall any State deprive any person of life, liberty, or property, without due process of law"). The court ruled against the butchers. It said that the due-process clause applied to rights connected to national, not state, citizenship. Though the plaintiffs were white, the ruling set a precedent that would be especially damaging to blacks. As long as the Supreme Court maintained a strict constructionist view of the Fourteenth Amendment—that is, focused on the letter of the law versus the spirit—it would not intervene when states created laws that basically nullified the newly won civil rights of blacks.

In late March 1876, the U.S. Supreme Court decided on a case rooted in the Colfax massacre of 1873 (*U.S. v. Cruikshank*). Several miscreants had in fact not gone "unwhipped of justice." They had been tried and found guilty in a federal court of violating one of the "force" acts created to stifle white terrorist groups. The Supreme Court overturned the convictions. Chief Justice Morrison Waite said force acts were invalid in prosecuting individuals for crimes against other individuals, that the federal government could avenge violations of people's rights only when the perpetrator was a state. Only local and state authorities could prosecute people for crimes against other people. As historian Eric Foner put it, the ruling "gave a green light to acts of terror where local officials either could not or would not enforce the law."

The court also handed down its decision in *U.S. v. Reese* in March 1876. This case turned on a Kentucky suffrage tax designed to keep blacks from voting. The court ruled that the Fifteenth Amendment didn't guarantee anyone the right to vote, but only prevented the denial of the vote because of "race, color, or previous condition of servitude." States were free to keep people from voting on other bases if they pleased. The ruling emboldened racist white lawmakers to devise lawsuit-proof ways to keep black men from voting.

But the Texan who wrote to *Harper's Weekly* was not talking about those Supreme Court cases. He took aim at Southern courts that "indict, convict, and sentence, for petty or pretended offenses, hundreds of colored men to serve out long terms of imprisonment at hard labor in the penitentiaries of the States." He cited a Texas prison inspector's report from some time back. According to the report, about thirteen hundred convicts had been "hired out to planters and railway contractors. Nearly all convicts employed on farms and railroads are Negroes." The sixteen-mile Overton-Henderson line was a railroad they worked on, "daylight until dark," dying at a rapid rate "owing to bad food and other causes."

Lake Jackson Plantation (sugarcane) in Brazoria County had the benefit of prison labor. There, convicts' quarters were "filled with vermin"; straw mattresses were their only bedding, whatever the weather. Floggings were frequent. Escapes from this hell on earth were few. Cause: Bloodhounds.

It was déjà vu. "Here," wrote the Texan, "the old slave plantations are worked with slaves again, and the old familiar hissing sound of the lash or the bull-whip . . . is once more heard; here, in this centennial year of our glorious supposed land of liberty, may again be heard the fierce howl of the bloodhound while in pursuit of a terrified escaped negro. Ah, how truly history repeats itself."

The Texan recalled the New Orleans and Memphis "tragedies of 1866" and the "recent butchery at Hamburg." If Democrats won the presidency in the upcoming election, there would be a bloodbath, he predicted. Groups like the KKK would "turn loose their bands of assassins and bloodhounds, and begin anew their carnivals of crime." The newspaper added a note: the man had asked that his name not be printed because "he believes that if his name were known he would be assassinated."

The Democratic Party's candidates for president and vice president in 1876 were New York governor Samuel Tilden and Indiana governor Thomas Hendricks. Tilden had made a name for himself in the mid-1860s as an anti-corruption crusader—most notably for his role in bringing down the Empire State's notorious "Boss" Tweed.

The Republican Party fielded former Ohio representative and governor Rutherford Hayes. Early on in his political career, Hayes had thrown in hard with the radicals, Thad Stevens among his idols. Over the years, Hayes had become more conservative. He and his running mate, New York representative William Wheeler, were in the camp that felt that the federal government was "governing the South too much."

The Republican Party of 1876 was radically different from the Republican Party of 1866. Firebrand Thad Stevens was dead. Stalwart Charles Sumner was dead. Ben Wade had retired from the Senate. Ben "the Beast" Butler had not won reelection in 1874 and soon defected to the Democratic Party. The Freedmen's Bureau had been phased out in 1872. At the Republican Party's national convention in Cincinnati, Ohio, Fred Douglass had been a lone voice crying in the wilderness.

"Do you mean to make good to us the promises in your constitution?" Douglass had asked. "You say you have emancipated us. You have: and I thank you for it. You say you have enfranchised us. You have: and I thank you for it. But what is your emancipation?—what is your enfranchisement? What does it all amount to, if the black man, after having been made free

Former congressman and New York state senator William Magear "Boss" Tweed (Democrat), who lorded over a ring of embezzling and bribe-taking politicians. Tweed specialized in kickbacks in exchange for contracts for construction projects, including a mammoth one that started in January 1870: the Brooklyn Bridge.

by the letter of your law, is unable to exercise that freedom?" Douglass's speech had done nothing to push Republicans onto a radical path. Still, he campaigned for Hayes.

Hayes and Tilden comported themselves with dignity during the campaign. Some of their supporters, however, did not. The pro-Hayes *New York Times* ran an article smearing Tilden as a tax cheat. Several days later, the pro-Tilden *Chicago Times* rolled out a story alleging that Hayes had slacked on filing taxes several years back. Some politicos who stumped for Hayes resorted to "waving the bloody shirt": whipping up hatred against the Democratic Party as the root cause of the Civil War.

"I am opposed to the Democratic Party, and I will tell you why," said the electric Roger Ingersoll, a former Union Army officer. Ingersoll was addressing veterans in Indianapolis in September 1876. "Every ordinance of secession that was drawn was drawn by a Democrat. . . . Every man that tried to destroy this nation was a Democrat. . . . Every man that shot Union soldiers was a Democrat. . . . Every man that loved slavery better than liberty was a Democrat. The man that assassinated Abraham Lincoln was a Democrat. Every man that raised bloodhounds to pursue human beings was a Democrat. Soldiers, every scar you have on your heroic bodies was given you by a Democrat."

About two weeks before Election Day, to the horror of Ingersoll and other Republicans, it looked like the next president would be a Democrat. Tilden was clearly the front-runner.

From the November 9, 1876, issue of the **Connecticut Courant**.

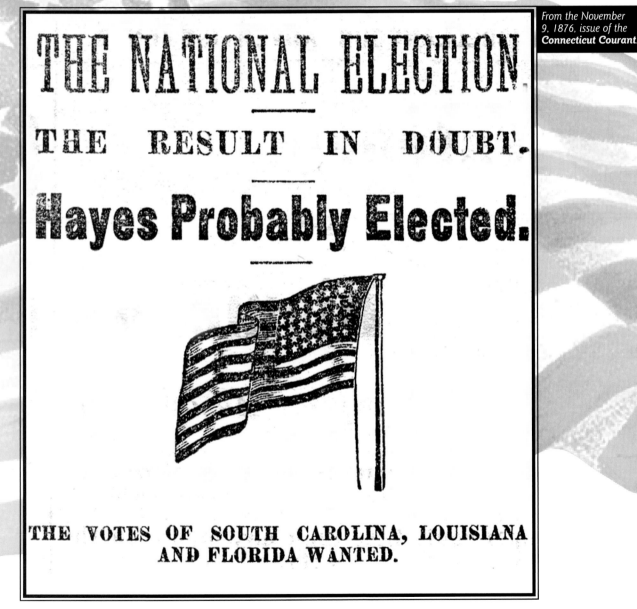

THE NATIONAL ELECTION.

THE RESULT IN DOUBT.

Hayes Probably Elected.

THE VOTES OF SOUTH CAROLINA, LOUISIANA AND FLORIDA WANTED.

"VICTORY!—Rousing Democratic Gains Everywhere—Tilden Next President!" blared the *Evening Gazette* of Port Jervis, New York, on November 8, the day after the election. "Complete Democratic Victory," echoed the *New York Tribune*. In contrast, the *New York Times* headlined one of its articles "A Doubtful Election."

Of the 369 electoral votes, 349 were booked. In Hayes's column, 165; in Tilden's, 184—plus he had about a quarter-million lead in the popular vote. But to win, Tilden needed 185 electoral votes. Most of the unaccounted-for 20 electoral votes belonged to three Southern states: Florida, Louisiana, and South Carolina. Each party claimed that their electors had won. Each side proclaimed the other's returns invalid because of fraud, from ballot-box stuffing to ballot-box destruction. Republicans charged Democrats with terrorizing blacks away from the polls.

The same charges and countercharges were in play for local and state offices. In South Carolina and Louisiana, Republicans bunkered in their statehouses with federal troops on guard. Democrats set up rival governments elsewhere. In Florida, the dispute between the Republican incumbent governor and the Democratic challenger ended up in its Democrat-dominated supreme court. The court gave the victory to the Democrat.

Oregon added to the drama when it was revealed that one of its three electors (all Republican-pledged) was illegitimate. He was a postmaster; according to the Constitution, federal employees cannot be electors. The error resulted in two sets of returns from the Beaver State.

The electoral colleges of the thirty-eight states were scheduled to convene on December 6 for the official tally of electors' votes. The nation rumbled regarding what to do about the twenty in dispute. "Tilden or War!" some Democrats roared. Stories of men dusting off uniforms and stocking up on ammunition juddered across telegraph wires. Acid fear of another civil war had prompted President Grant to bulk up troop presence in D.C.

December 6 . . . Christmas . . . New Year's Eve. The centennial year went and still no president. When groundhogs checked for shadows, still no clue. During the wait, Congress had created an Electoral Commission of congressmen and Supreme Court justices—eight Republicans, seven Democrats—to investigate the stories behind the disputed returns.

Many historians call the outcome the "Compromise" or the "Bargain" of 1877, a deal that satisfied the wants of powerful whites. It included pledges that certain people would receive cabinet posts and other federal appointments and that the South would receive federal funds for

"The negroes of the South are free—free as air," says the parliamentary Watterson. This is what the *State*, a well-known Democratic organ of Tennessee, says, in huge capitals, on the subject: "Let it be known before the election that the farmers have agreed to spot every leading Radical negro in the county, and treat him as an enemy for all time to come. The rotten ring must and shall be broken at any and all costs. The Democrats have determined to withdraw all employment from their enemies. Let this fact be known."

*Voter intimidation was raw and rampant. This A. B. Furst illustration ran in the October 21, 1876, issue of **Harper's Weekly**, captioned "OF COURSE HE WANTS TO VOTE THE DEMOCRATIC TICKET!"*

building up its infrastructure, especially its railroads. Above all, Democrats wanted control of politics in the South. Above all, Republicans wanted the presidency. General Sherman, whom Grant had made general-in-chief of the army, didn't want troops tied up in the South. He wanted maximum manpower to fulfill his long-ago proclamation that Native Americans not living on reservations were automatically "hostile and will remain so until killed off." Some contend that there was no bargain, no compromise at all. Rather, when, on March 2, 1877, following a vote of 8–7, the Electoral Commission proclaimed Rutherford Hayes president, it did so based on a fair, impartial assessment of the facts.

One of the first things President Hayes did was recognize the

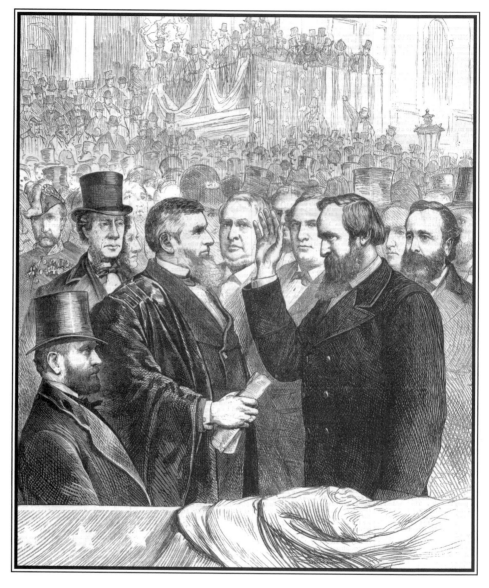

*From the cover of the March 24, 1877, issue of **Harper's Weekly**. U.S. Supreme Court Chief Justice Morrison Waite administers the oath of office to Rutherford Birchard Hayes at the Capitol Building on March 5, 1877. Few people knew that Hayes was already legally the nation's nineteenth president. On March 3, the day after the Electoral Commission declared Hayes the victor, Waite had performed a secret swearing-in at the Executive Mansion. There had been talk of an assassination plot. Were Hayes to be killed after March 3, the presidency wouldn't be out of Republican control. "I felt like a boy getting out of school," Grant (in profile wearing top hat) later said of the day he left office.*

Democratic contenders as the rightful winners in the South Carolina and Louisiana gubernatorial races. Troops guarding their statehouses were ordered to stand down. Southern Republicans were on their own as the Hayes administration eyeballed the economy.

"The Tramp has become a recognized institution of the country," the *American Socialist* had griped in the fall of 1876. "They pillage farm-houses, plunder hamlets, and stop railroad trains." The newspaper, published by a commune in Oneida, New York, argued that the solution to this "great and growing evil" was to abandon the concept of family based on biology and embrace communal living. What most working-class people cried out for was, *Jobs! Jobs! Jobs!—and higher wages!*

Layoffs, wage cuts—companies had continued tightening their belts. Then, when the Baltimore and Ohio Railroad rammed through another wage cut (10 percent) in mid-July 1877, B&O brakemen, firemen, and engineers went on what became the Great Strike. "Great" because other railroad workers around the nation went on a sympathy strike. "Great" because factory workers, coal miners, and other low-wage workers followed suit. Workers not only went off work, they went wild, with the unemployed in the mix. News flash—*Sabotage!* News flash—*Arson!* News flash—*Looting!* Police and the people battled in the streets. Governors called up militias; President Hayes dispatched troops to the worst trouble spots. Civilians' pistols, bricks, and other makeshift weapons were no match for soldiers' Springfield rifles and Gatling guns.

"Scenes of riot and bloodshed accompanied [the strike] such as we have never before witnessed in the uprising of labor against capital," reported *Harper's Weekly* on August 11. "Commerce has been obstructed, industries have been paralyzed, hundreds of lives sacrificed, and millions of dollars' worth of property destroyed by lawless mobs."

*"There is no greater folly than to say that the tramp is a laborer or artisan out of employ, and looking for work," insisted the article that accompanied this engraving (**Harper's Weekly**, September 2, 1876). Readers were schooled on the difference between "honest and earnest" unemployed people (deserving of occasional charity) and "dangerous stragglers," the "peregrinating scoundrels," the "true, genuine tramp."*

On Baltimore Street in Baltimore, Maryland, militiamen make their way to Camden Station.

At the end of the article, the newspaper made quick mention of recent lawlessness in California. In late July, an "immense anti-Chinese mob" had savaged San Francisco's Chinatown. This was neither the first nor the last such riot of the era. Cause: By working as gardeners and housekeepers and in other jobs for wages lower than whites would accept, the Chinese were taking "the bread out of the mouths of the white men and their families," charged an organization in Gold Run, California. The group pledged to rid the nation of a people they called "a detriment and a curse to our country."

"THE FRENZY, AND WHAT CAME OF IT," from the cover of the August 18, 1877, issue of *Harper's Weekly*, which carried a follow-up article on the Great Strike.

Twelve years after the Civil War ended, on certain fronts America was still an absolute mess, and the words Andy Johnson had uttered at war's end were true: "There is no such thing as Reconstruction."

In 1879, newspapers began reporting on a black exodus from the South. By spring 1879, about five thousand had left Mississippi and Louisiana. In this engraving from the April 19, 1879, issue of **Frank Leslie's Illustrated Newspaper**, a pastor and some of his parishioners in St. Louis, Missouri, greet recent arrivals from the Deep South. Local churches fed and sheltered the travelers, most of whom were on their way to where land was cheap and plentiful: to Kansas and elsewhere in the West, in some cases creating all-black towns. Exodusters, they were called. Most were agricultural workers. All wanted to live where "freedom was a reality, not a shadow," as one newspaper put it. Only thousands, not millions, of blacks left the South immediately after the demise of Congressional Reconstruction. Just as during the days of slavery, the South remained where the majority of blacks lived.

Eric Foner subtitled his book on Reconstruction *America's Unfinished Revolution*. Another historian, Hans Trefousse, chose *America's First Effort at Racial Democracy*.

Reconstruction was a time of enormous possibilities. As the nation was remaking itself, it could have looked hard at its founding document, the Declaration of Independence, and taken to heart its most oft-quoted passage: "We hold these truths to be self-evident, that all men are created equal, that they are endowed by their Creator with certain unalienable Rights, that among these are Life, Liberty and the pursuit of Happiness." For starters, the nation could have said, let us agree that "all men" is just shorthand for *everybody*. But there was no national will for this. Instead, America settled for being a "white man's country" that let "white men rule."

Had America been righteous, there would have been a halt to the assault on Native Americans and no march of massacres, climaxing with the one near South Dakota's Wounded Knee Creek in 1890. Captains of industry would have realized that respected workers, workers who received decent wages, would be better workers and more productive members of society. And women would not have had to wait until 1920 to get the right to vote nationally.

Congress would not have enacted a series of laws, beginning in 1882, that banned for decades Chinese immigration and barred the Chinese in America from becoming naturalized citizens. Not so for people from certain other countries, many of whom shed their accents and other telltale signs of their culture to join the ranks of the Americans the nation said were the only ones who *really* mattered. What James Baldwin wrote of the twentieth century in his essay "The Price of the Ticket" applied to earlier times: "They come through Ellis Island, where *Giorgio* becomes *Joe*, *Papavasiliou* becomes *Palmer*, *Evangelos* becomes *Evans*, *Goldsmith* becomes *Smith* or *Gold*, and *Avakian* becomes *King*. So, with a painless change of name, and in the twinkling of an eye, one becomes a white American." Baldwin acknowledged that the process may not have remained painless. "Later, in the midnight hour, the missing identity aches."

For blacks who chose not to or could not pass for white, America was a mean place to be after Reconstruction. Loopholes in the Fifteenth Amendment were maximized: poll taxes and literacy tests abounded, disenfranchising a lot of poor whites along with a multitude of blacks. In 1883, the U.S. Supreme Court killed the Civil Rights Act of 1875. The court said that the passage on equality of access to public accommodation was unconstitutional. The ruling condoned "colored only" and "white only" signs and attitudes in public places, and other manifestations of second-class citizenship for blacks, all over the nation. Segregation became the legally entrenched American way with the U.S. Supreme Court's 1896 ruling in *Plessy v. Ferguson.* The court said separate facilities for blacks and whites were legitimate so long as they were equal. They never were and never would be, but the majority of Americans didn't seem to care. Inequality, coupled with white-on-black violence, doomed millions of blacks to poverty. Still, so many hoped, strived, and prayed.

In the early twentieth century, blacks soldiered on for justice and equal opportunity. Leaders included the Mississippi-born antilynching activist Ida Wells-Barnett, whose parents had been Republican Party loyalists. Another was the historian who called Reconstruction a "splendid failure," William Edward Burghardt Du Bois, the first black person to earn a Ph.D. from Harvard University (1896) and co-founder (1909) of the National Association for the Advancement of Colored People (NAACP). Du Bois, a child during Reconstruction, owed some of his success to such Reconstruction-spawned institutions as Fisk University, his first alma mater.

After decades of civil rights crusading by the NAACP and other organizations, about eighty years after Reconstruction ended, hope for major social change surged. The milestone date: May 17, 1954, the day the U.S. Supreme Court ruled in the public school desegregation case known in short as *Brown v. Board of Education.* The court declared the separate-but-equal doctrine unconstitutional. The ruling overturned the *Plessy* decision, based on a broad interpretation of a passage of Reconstruction-era legislation: the Fourteenth Amendment's equal-protection clause. The *Brown* decision marked the start of the end of government-sanctioned segregation at least.

The campaign for black civil rights in the 1950s and 1960s led to legislation that benefited an array of Americans. Chiefly, the Civil Rights Act of 1964, which outlawed poll taxes and other impediments to voting. It also outlawed discrimination in housing, jobs, and other arenas of life for all people who were not white. This groundbreaking legislation was heartily supported and signed into law by the nation's second President Johnson: Lyndon Baines Johnson, a Southerner and a Democrat. The make-up and the agendas of the two main political parties were in flux. And on the wings of black activism, women and other groups stepped up their campaigns for respect and equal opportunity.

People call this era the Second Reconstruction. Many contend that, like the first, it also went unfinished and that the twenty-first century dawned on an American democracy still under construction. Some Americans hoped for a Third Reconstruction, but the majority apparently saw no need, no cause.

PROLOGUE

Dates for Reconstruction. Some historians use 1865 as Reconstruction's start date. Like others, I choose 1863 because of Lincoln's Reconstruction initiative that year.
"had no . . . respect." Taney, who wrote the majority opinion of the Court in *Dred Scott v. Sanford*, March 6, 1857. Reprinted in Finkelman, *Dred Scott v. Sanford*, p. 61.

CHAPTER 1:
"TRAITORS MUST BE PUNISHED"

"They shall . . . this." Johnson, quoted in Trefousse, *Andrew Johnson*, p. 194.
"Some day . . . sweat of the brow." Johnson, quoted in S. Mintz, "Should Andrew Johnson Have Been Impeached?" (2003), Digital History, www.digitalhistory.uh.edu.
"We feel . . . alone." Davis, reprinted in Gienapp, ed., *The Civil War and Reconstruction*, pp. 72–73.
"I believe . . . free." Lincoln, "House Divided" speech, June 16, 1858, quoted in Wagner et al., eds., *The Library of Congress Civil War Desk Reference*, p. 116.
South Carolina Ordinance of Secession. *The (Philadelphia) Press*, December 21, 1860, p. 2.
"Treason must . . . impoverished," "Their great . . . men," and **"ought to be hung."** Johnson, quoted in Simpson, *The Reconstruction Presidents*, p. 68.

CHAPTER 2:
"TO A FAIRER FUTURE OF LIBERTY AND PEACE"

Lincoln's Ten Percent Plan. Reprinted in Trefousse, *Reconstruction*, pp. 83–86.
"war for . . . Union" and **"Moses" speech.** Johnson, quoted in Trefousse, *Andrew Johnson*, pp. 135, 183.
"Can't you . . . for one?" Stevens, quoted in Trefousse, *Thaddeus Stevens*, p. 146.
"a damn scoundrel." Stevens, quoted in Trefousse, *Andrew Johnson*, p. 180.
Douglass's memory of Johnson on Inauguration Day. Douglass, *Frederick Douglass: Autobiographies*, p. 802.
End of the Civil War. Some Confederate forces continued to fight after Lee's surrender. It would be several weeks before all Confederate soldiers surrendered, and not until November 1865 that the last of the CSA's naval units did so.
Lincoln's speech of April 11, 1865. Accessed at Project Gutenberg, www.gutenberg.org.
"That means . . . citizenship," "Sic semper tyrannis!" and **"The South shall be free!"** Booth, quoted in Kauffman, *American Brutus*, pp. 7, 210.

CHAPTER 3:
"JOHNSON, WE HAVE FAITH IN YOU"

"The stench . . . ground." Oates, quoted in Ward, *The Civil War*, p. 295.
Hodges's "information wanted" ad. *The Christian Recorder*, August 20, 1870, retrieved at Accessible Archives, www.accessible.com.
On the Louisville "rebel she." *The New York Times*, May 16, 1865, p. 8.
"Johnson, we . . . government." Wade, quoted in Trefousse, *Andrew Johnson*, p. 197.
"generally agree . . . cruelty." Wagner et al., eds., *The Library of Congress Civil War Desk Reference*, p. 609.
Johnson's Proclamation of Amnesty and North Carolina Proclamation. Reprinted in Trefousse, *Reconstruction*, pp. 90–92, 93–96.
Wade-Davis manifesto. Reprinted in Gienapp, ed., *The Civil War and Reconstruction*, pp. 318–319.
"Their life . . . suspended" and **"There is no . . . reconstruction."** Johnson, quoted in Simpson, *The Reconstruction Presidents*, pp. 69, 75.
Confederate debt estimate. Foner, *A Short History of Reconstruction*, p. 91.
"call your . . . 'Master.'" Marvin, quoted in Foner, *Reconstruction*, p. 189.
Jourdon Anderson's letter. Reprinted in Gienapp, ed., *The Civil War and Reconstruction*, pp. 380–381.

CHAPTER 4:
"THIS IS A COUNTRY FOR WHITE MEN"

On Slabtown. *Harper's Weekly*, September 30, 1865, p. 613.
"This is . . . white men." Johnson, quoted in Trefousse, *Andrew Johnson*, p. 236.
"Is there no . . . President?" Stevens, quoted in Trefousse, *Andrew Johnson*, p. 217.
Mississippi Black Codes. Posted at www.usconstitution.com/blackcodesofmississippi.htm.
"It was . . . to learn." Washington, *Up from Slavery*, p. 30.
"qualities . . . social reformer." W.E.B. Du Bois, *Black Reconstruction in America*, p. 223.
Letter from 36th Regiment. Sergeant Richard Etheredge and William Benson, reprinted in
Berlin and Rowland, eds., *Families and Freedom*, pp. 125–126.
"Why . . . not right!" Unidentified man, quoted in Howard, *Autobiography*, pp. 238–239.
"lay aside . . . masters" and "You ask . . . forgive." Howard and unidentified man,
quoted in Foner, *Reconstruction*, p. 160.
Estimate on black loss of land. Foner, *Reconstruction*, p. 164.
"We do . . . citizenship." *Equal Suffrage. Address from the Colored Citizens of Norfolk, VA.,
to the People of the United States* (New Bedford, MA: E. Anthony & Sons, 1865), p. 1.
"Our new . . . condition." Stephens, www.usconstitution.com/cornerstonespeech.htm.

CHAPTER 5:
"A BLOW TO OUR GOVERNMENT SYSTEM"

"A blow to . . . system." Welles, quoted in Leonard, *Lincoln's Avengers*, p. 197.
Petitions of Raymond and Lawrence and resolution of Moulton on December 18, 1865.
House Journal, 39th Congress, 1st session, 1865, pp. 73, 74, 78.
Stevens's speech. *Congressional Globe*, 39th Congress, 1st session, pp. 72–75.
South Carolina census data. Retrieved from Historical Census Browser,
http://fisher.lib.virginia.edu/collections/stats/histcensus/index.html.
"The ensuing . . . democracy." Du Bois, *Black Reconstruction in America*, pp. 266–267.

CHAPTER 6:
"WE ARE AMERICANS"

"If it is . . . giants." Sherman, quoted in *The Railroad Photographs of Alfred A. Hart, Artist*,
by Mead B. Kibbey. Posted at Central Pacific Railroad Photographic History Museum,
http://cprr.org/Museum/index.html.
"Slavery . . . the ballot," Douglass, and "teach . . . justice," Dickinson. *The New York
Times*, May 11, 1865, p. 2.
On black delegation to the White House and other news. *Providence Evening Press*,
February 8, 1866, pp. 1, 3.
"I know . . . nigger." Johnson, quoted in Trefousse, *Andrew Johnson*, p. 242.
Freedmen's Bureau bill. McPherson, *The Political History*, pp. 72–74.
Johnson's veto of the Freedmen's Bureau bill. McPherson, *The Political History*, pp. 72–74.
1866 civil rights bill. Reprinted in Blaustein and Zangrando, *Civil Rights and African Americans*,
pp. 229–232.
Johnson's veto of the civil rights bill. *Journal of the Senate*, vol. 58, pp. 279–285.
New York Times report on Memphis riot. Reprinted in *Harper's Weekly*, May 26, 1866,
cover.

CHAPTER 7:
"CAUSE"

On murders and outrages in Texas, Tennessee, Louisiana, and Maryland. Records of the
Assistant Commissioner for the State of Texas, Records of the Assistant Commissioner for

the State of Tennessee, Records of the Assistant Commissioner for the State of Louisiana, Records of the Assistant Commissioner for the District of Columbia, www.freedmensbureau.com.

Beeby's letter. Records of the Assistant Commissioner for the State of South Carolina, www.freedmensbureau.com.

Clara Barton's testimony. *Report of the Joint Committee on Reconstruction*, 1866, posted at www.adena.com.

Rufus Saxton's testimony. Posted at S. Mintz (2003), Digital History, www.digitalhistory.uh.edu.

CHAPTER 8:
"WHY NOT HANG THAD STEVENS!"

Alfred Waud's account of Unionist meeting. *Harper's Weekly*, August 4, 1866, pp. 485–486.

Tarbell's testimony. Posted at www.adena.com.

"Traitors to Their Race" article and circulation claim. *The New York Day-Book*, July 7, 1866, p. 4.

"an absolute massacre." Sheridan, quoted in Foner, *Reconstruction*, p. 263.

Samuel Cox on terrorism. Cox, *Three Decades of Federal Legislation*, p. 453.

Johnson's speech in Cleveland. September 3, 1866. Posted at "From Revolution to Reconstruction," http://odur.let.rug.nl/~usa/D/1851-1875/reconstruction/cleveland.htm.

On Johnson and crowds during tour. Trefousse, *Andrew Johnson*, pp. 262–268.

"Depend upon . . . helps." Quoted in Trefousse, *Andrew Johnson*, p. 264.

CHAPTER 9:
"MAKING A WHIPPING-POST OF THE SOUTH"

"We are . . . nation." Stevens, *Congressional Globe*, 40th Congress, 2nd session, p. 1966.

On black men voting in Georgetown. *Harper's Weekly*, March 16, 1867, p. 162.

Acts pertaining to cemeteries and waterways. *Statutes at Large*, 39th Congress, 2nd session, pp. 399–401, 418–422.

Acts on the franchise in D.C., Johnson's pardon powers, the franchise in the territories, and the creation of Howard University. *Statutes at Large*, 39th Congress, 2nd session, pp. 375–376, 377, 379–381, 438–439.

Tenure of Office Act. McPherson, *The Political History*, pp. 176–177.

"to protect niggers." Johnson to Charles Nordhoff, managing editor of the *New York Evening Post*, quoted in Simpson, *The Reconstruction Presidents*, p. 114.

Johnson's veto of first Reconstruction bill. *House Journal*, pp. 563–572.

First, Second, and Third Reconstruction Acts. Reprinted in Trefousse, *Reconstruction*, pp. 111–113, 114–117, 118–121.

"The punishment . . . sluggish Congress." Stevens, *Congressional Globe*, 40th Congress, 1st session, p. 203.

H.R. 29. *House Bills and Resolutions*, 40th Congress, 1st session, pp. 1–5.

"making a . . . South." Taylor, *Destruction and Reconstruction*, p. 255.

CHAPTER 10:
"WE ARE WISE ENOUGH"

"We are . . . citizen." Berry, quoted in Foner, *Freedom's Lawmakers*, p. 18.

"convictions of . . . soul." Lynch, quoted in Foner, *Freedom's Lawmakers*, p. 138.

On "The First Vote." *Harper's Weekly*, November 16, 1867, p. 722.

"I make . . . all my writings." Colby, quoted in Foner, *Freedom's Lawmakers*, p. xxiv.

"I acknowledge . . . enjoy?" Whipper, quoted in Sterling, ed., *The Trouble They Seen*, p. 134.

CHAPTER 11:
"THE GREAT OBSTRUCTION"

Alaska Treaty. Posted at the Avalon Project at Yale University, www.yale.edu/lawweb/avalon/diplomacy/russia/treatywi.htm.

Medicine Lodge Treaty. Posted at www.comanchelodge.com/medicine.htm.

"We took . . . less?" Sheridan, quoted in "Tragedy of the Plains." Posted at S. Mintz (2003), Digital History, www.digitalhistory.uh.edu.

"What . . . into Johnson?" (G. W. Patterson to Thurlow Weed, August 21, 1867); **"Fathers . . . Equality";** and Bowles's letter to Shellabarger. Trefousse, *Impeachment of a President*, pp. 83, 88, 94.

Johnson's December 3, 1867, Annual Message. Posted at "State of the Union Messages," The American Presidency Project, www.presidency.ucsb.edu.

"the great obstruction." Stevens, quoted in Trefousse, *Impeachment of a President*, p. 51.

CHAPTER 12:
"OR OTHER HIGH CRIMES AND MISDEMEANORS"

"We believe . . . treason." *Chicago Tribune*, March 31, 1866, quoted in Trefousse, *Impeachment of a President*, p. 48.

"A greater reprobate . . . chair." T.W.C., "Impeachment," *The Christian Recorder*, January 19, 1867. Retrieved from Accessible Archives, www.accessible.com.

"by virtue of . . . United States," Johnson; **"Stick,"** Sumner; and **"Didn't I . . . kill you."** Stevens, quoted in Trefousse, *Impeachment of a President*, pp. 134, 135.

Articles of impeachment. Reprinted in Trefousse, *Reconstruction*, pp. 122–134.

Vote on Article XI. *Senate Journal*, pp. 941–944.

"What was the verdict?" and **"The country . . . devil!"** Spectator and Stevens, quoted in Trefousse, *Thaddeus Stevens*, p. 234.

"It is impossible . . . South" and **"News . . . 'lost cause.'"** George E. Spencer and Daniel Richards, quoted in Trefousse, *Andrew Johnson*, p. 333.

"governed by . . . character." Trumbull, "Opinion," posted at "Famous Trials," www.law.umkc.edu/faculty/projects/ftrials/ftrials.htm.

CHAPTER 13:
"THE BILL DO PASS"

"Resolved . . . the same." *Statutes at Large*, 40th Congress, 2nd session, p. 73.

South Carolina petition. Reprinted in Gienapp, ed., *The Civil War and Reconstruction*, pp. 369–370.

"bill do pass." *Statutes at Large*, 40th Congress, 2nd session, p. 74.

Fourteenth Amendment. Reprinted in Gienapp, ed., *The Civil War and Reconstruction*, pp. 427–428.

Stevens's epitaph. Quoted in Carter G. Woodson, "Thaddeus Stevens," *Negro History Bulletin*, December 1949, p. 52.

***Planters' Banner* article.** Reprinted in Ferrell, *Reconstruction*, p. 173.

CHAPTER 14:
"LET US HAVE PEACE"

Grant's acceptance letter. Posted at Ulysses S. Grant Network, www.css.edu/usgrant.

"The Republican . . . time." Gillette, *Retreat from Reconstruction*, p. 19.

"Think of . . . education," Elizabeth Cady Stanton; and exchanges at 1869 AERA convention. Quoted in Ward and Burns, *Not for Ourselves Alone*, pp. 116, 119–120.

"East and West . . . Continent." *The New York Times*, May 11, 1969, p. 1.

CHAPTER 15:
"ON ACCOUNT OF RACE, COLOR, OR PREVIOUS CONDITION OF SERVITUDE"

"These cars . . . continent." *Harper's Weekly*, May 29, 1869, p. 342.

"I have . . . my life." Cornelius Vanderbilt, quoted at www.nps.gov/vama/house_of.html.

"contribute . . . common country." Cornelius Vanderbilt, quoted at www.vanderbilt.edu/admissions/history.htm.

"I speak . . . whole country." Myers, quoted in the *New York Times*, August 19, 1869, reprinted in Aptheker, ed., *A Documentary History of the Negro People in the United States*, pp. 628–629.

"In our . . . color." CNLU Address, *The New Era*, January 13, 1870, reprinted in Aptheker, ed., *A Documentary History of the Negro People in the United States*, p. 632.

Greene County population. According to the 1860 census, of Greene County's total population of 12,652 people, there were 4,229 whites, 25 free blacks, and 8,398 enslaved people. In the 1870 census of a total population of 12,454, there were 4,298 whites and 8,156 blacks. Historical Census Browser, http://fisher.lib.virginia.edu/collections/stats/histcensus/index.html.

Colby's recollection of beating. Quoted in Foner, *Freedom's Lawmakers*, p. 48. My search for an image of Colby was unsuccessful.

CHAPTER 16:
"WE ARE GOVERNING THE SOUTH TOO MUCH"

Questions for KKK candidates. Reprinted in Ferrell, *Reconstruction*, p. 184.

Force acts. Reprinted in Trefousse, *Reconstruction*, pp. 154–175.

On writ of *habeas corpus*. If a person was jailed without charge, a judge could issue a writ (order) of *habeas corpus*, forcing the authority holding someone in custody to bring the person before the court. During the Civil War, as allowed in the U.S. Constitution, Abraham Lincoln had suspended the writ of *habeas corpus* so that Union authorities could freely lock up people in the North and Border States they deemed disloyal and a danger to the Union (about twenty thousand people were jailed under this measure).

South Carolinian's letter and remarks on martial law. *Walla Walla Statesman*, November 25, 1871, pp. 1, 2.

Farnsworth's speech. *Congressional Globe*, appendix, 42nd Congress, 1st session, pp. 116–117.

Article on the KKK. Eugene Lawrence, *Harper's Weekly*, October 19, 1872, p. 805.

Betsey Westbrook's testimony. Reprinted in Sterling, ed., *The Trouble They Seen*, pp. 390–391.

CHAPTER 17:
"ALL WE WANT IS TO LIVE UNDER THE LAW"

"An important question . . . Anthony" and **"Concerning Women" column.** Unsigned article, *The Woman's Journal*, January 25, 1873, p. 25.

"simple . . . forgotten." Unidentified person, quoted in David C. Bartlett and Larry A. McClellan, "The Final Ministry of Amanda Berry Smith: An Orphanage in Harvey, Illinois, 1895–1918," posted at www.lib.niu.edu/ipo/ihwt9820.html.

"The Louisiana . . . Wounded." *Harper's Weekly*, May 10, 1873, p. 396.

"extended up . . . polls" and **"We could . . . law."** Foner, *Reconstruction*, pp. 436, 437.

"The Financial Flurry" article and "Social Gossip" column. *The Daily Critic*, September 30, 1873, pp. 1, 3.

CHAPTER 18:
"WHY IS THIS, MA?"

"the only British . . . America." Lamson, *The Glorious Failure*, p. 30.

Robert Elliott's January 6, 1874, speech. *Congressional Record*, 43rd Congress, 1st session, pp. 407–410.

"There is . . . our feet." Sumner, quoted in Du Bois, *Black Reconstruction in America*, pp. 592–593.

"the very men . . . outrages." Long, quoted in Foner, *Freedom's Lawmakers*, p. 136.

Sarah Thompson's letter to Sumner. Reprinted in Sterling, ed., *We Are Your Sisters*, p. 363.

On aftermath of Freedman's Bank collapse. "The Freedman's Savings and Trust Company and African American Genealogical Research" by Reginald Washington in *Prologue*, Summer 1997. Posted at www.archives.gov/publications/prologue/1997/summer/freedmans-savings-and-trust.html.

"Fierce denunciations . . . punished." Grant, *Senate Journal*, pp. 103–110.

Civil Rights Act of 1875. Reprinted in Blaustein and Zangrando, *Civil Rights and African Americans*, pp. 241–243.

CHAPTER 19:
"THE PROMISES IN YOUR CONSTITUTION"

Independence Day ceremonies. The man presiding at Independence Hall was Thomas Ferry, president *pro tem* of the Senate and acting vice president. Vice President Henry Wilson had died in November 1875.

"We ask . . . forever." Anthony, quoted in Ward and Burns, *Not for Ourselves Alone*, p. 153.

"This is . . . South Carolina." Dock Adams, quoted in Foner, *Reconstruction*, p. 572.

On China pavilion, and letter from a Texan. *Harper's Weekly*, September 2, 1876, pp. 718, 722.

"gave a . . . law." Foner, *Reconstruction*, p. 530.

Douglass's speech at RNC. Quoted in Gillette, *Retreat from Reconstruction*, p. 304.

Ingersoll's speech in Indianapolis. Quoted in Morris, *Fraud of the Century*, p. 141.

CHAPTER 20:
"A DOUBTFUL ELECTION"

"VICTORY! . . . President!" *Evening Gazette* (Port Jervis, New York), November 8, 1876, p. 1.

"Complete Democratic Victory." *New York Tribune*, quoted in Morris, *Fraud of the Century*, p. 164.

"A Doubtful Election." *The New York Times*, November 8, 1876, p. 4.

"hostile and . . . off." Sherman, quoted in www.pbs.org/weta/thewest/people/s_z/sherman.htm.

"I felt . . . school." Grant, quoted in Smith, *Grant*, p. 605.

"The Tramp . . . trains." "The Tramp Nuisance—Its Causes and Cure," *The American Socialist*, October 12, 1876, p. 228.

"There is . . . work." "The Tramp," *Harper's Weekly*, September 2, 1876, pp. 718–719.

"Scenes of . . . mobs." "The Great Strike," *Harper's Weekly*, August 11, 1877, p. 626.

EPILOGUE

"freedom . . . a shadow." *The New York Times*, March 18, 1879, quoted in Richardson, *The Death of Reconstruction*, p. 167.

"They . . . white American." Baldwin, *The Price of the Ticket*, p. xix.

"splendid failure." Du Bois, *Black Reconstruction in America*, p. 708.

SELECTED SOURCES

Aptheker, Herbert, ed. *A Documentary History of the Negro People in the United States.* Vol. 2. 1951. Reissue. Secaucus, NJ: Citadel Press, 1992.

Bain, David Haward. *Empire Express: Building the First Transcontinental Railroad.* New York: Penguin, 2000.

Baldwin, James. *The Price of the Ticket: Collected Nonfiction, 1948–1985.* New York: St. Martin's, 1985.

Berlin, Ira, and Leslie S. Rowland, eds. *Families and Freedom: A Documentary History of African-American Kinship in the Civil War Era.* New York: The New Press, 1997.

Blaustein, Albert P., and Robert L. Zangrando. *Civil Rights and African Americans: A Documentary History.* Evanston, IL: Northwestern University Press, 1991.

Cox, Samuel Sullivan. *Three Decades of Federal Legislation, 1855 to 1885.* Providence, RI: J. A. & R. A. Reid, 1885.

Douglass, Frederick. *Life and Times of Frederick Douglass.* 1881. Collected in *Frederick Douglass: Autobiographies.* New York: Library of America, 1994.

Du Bois, W.E.B. *Black Reconstruction in America: An Essay Toward a History of the Part Which Black Folk Played in the Attempt to Reconstruct Democracy in America, 1860–1880.* 1935. Reissue. New York: Russell & Russell, 1966.

Duncan, Russell. *Freedom's Shore: Tunis Campbell and the Georgia Freedmen.* Athens: University of Georgia Press, 1986.

Ferrell, Claudine L. *Reconstruction.* Westport, CT: Greenwood Press, 2003.

Finkelman, Paul. *Dred Scott v. Sanford: A Brief History with Documents.* Boston: Bedford Books, 1997.

Foner, Eric. *Freedom's Lawmakers: A Directory of Black Officeholders During Reconstruction.* Revised ed. Baton Rouge: Louisiana State University Press, 1996.

———. *Reconstruction: America's Unfinished Revolution, 1863–1877.* New York: Harper & Row, 1988.

———. *A Short History of Reconstruction, 1863–1877.* New York: Harper & Row, 1990.

Foner, Eric, and Olivia Mahoney. *America's Reconstruction: People and Politics After the Civil War.* Baton Rouge: Louisiana State University Press, 1997.

Gienapp, William E., ed. *The Civil War and Reconstruction: A Documentary Collection.* New York: W. W. Norton, 2001.

Gillette, William. *Retreat from Reconstruction, 1869–1879.* Baton Rouge: Louisiana State University Press, 1979.

Hirshson, Stanley P. *The White Tecumseh: A Biography of William T. Sherman.* New York: John Wiley & Sons, 1997.

Howard, Oliver Otis. *Autobiography of Oliver Otis Howard.* 1907. Reprint. Harrisburg, PA: The Archive Society, 1997.

Kauffman, Michael W. *American Brutus: John Wilkes Booth and the Lincoln Conspiracies.* New York: Random House, 2004.

Lamson, Peggy. *The Glorious Failure: Black Congressman Robert Brown Elliott and the Reconstruction in South Carolina.* New York: W. W. Norton, 1974.

Leonard, Elizabeth D. *Lincoln's Avengers: Justice, Revenge, and Reunion After the Civil War.* New York: W. W. Norton, 2004.

Lynch, John R. *The Facts of Reconstruction.* 1913. Reprint, edited with an introduction by William G. Harris. Indianapolis: Bobbs-Merrill, 1970.

McFeely, William S. *Frederick Douglass.* New York: W. W. Norton, 1991.

McPherson, Edward. *The Political History of the United States of America During the Period of Reconstruction.* 2nd ed. 1875. Reprint. New York: Negro Universities Press, 1969.

Morris, Roy, Jr. *Fraud of the Century: Rutherford B. Hayes, Samuel Tilden, and the Stolen Election of 1876.* New York: Simon & Schuster, 2003.

Richardson, Heather Cox. *The Death of Reconstruction: Race, Labor, and Politics in the Post–Civil War North, 1865–1901.* Cambridge, MA: Harvard University Press, 2004.

Simpson, Brooks D. *The Reconstruction Presidents.* Lawrence: University Press of Kansas, 1998.

Smith, Jean Edward. *Grant.* New York: Simon & Schuster, 2001.

Smith, John David. *Black Voices from Reconstruction, 1865–1877.* Gainesville: University Press of Florida, 1997.

Sterling, Dorothy, ed. *The Trouble They Seen: The Story of Reconstruction in the Words of African Americans.* New York: Da Capo Press, 1994.

———. *We Are Your Sisters: Black Women in the Nineteenth Century.* New York: W. W. Norton, 1984.

Taylor, Richard. *Destruction and Reconstruction: Personal Experiences of the Civil War.* 1879. Reprint, with a new introduction by T. Michael Parrish. New York: Da Capo Press, 1995.

Trefousse, Hans L. *Andrew Johnson: A Biography.* New York: W. W. Norton, 1997.

———. *Historical Dictionary of Reconstruction.* Westport, CT: Greenwood Press, 1991.

———. *Impeachment of a President: Andrew Johnson, the Blacks, and Reconstruction.* New York: Fordham University Press, 1999.

———. *Reconstruction: America's First Effort at Racial Democracy.* Updated ed. Malabar, FL: Krieger Publishing, 1999.

———. *Thaddeus Stevens: Nineteenth-Century Egalitarian.* Mechanicsburg, PA: Stackpole Books, 2001.

Wagner, Margaret E., Gary W. Gallagher, and Paul Finkelman, eds. *The Library of Congress Civil War Desk Reference.* New York: Simon & Schuster, 2002.

Ward, Geoffrey C., with Ric Burns and Ken Burns. *The Civil War.* New York: Knopf, 1992.

Ward, Geoffrey C., and Ken Burns. *Not for Ourselves Alone: The Story of Elizabeth Cady Stanton and Susan B. Anthony.* New York: Knopf, 1999.

Washington, Booker T. *Up from Slavery.* 1901. Reprint. New York: Penguin, 1986.

WGBH Boston Educational Foundation. *Reconstruction: The Second Civil War.* DVD. PBS Home Video, 2004.

———. *Ulysses S. Grant: Warrior, President.* VHS. PBS Home Video, 2002.

ILLUSTRATION CREDITS

All illustrations not credited below are from the author's collection.

Culver Pictures: p. 89 "Woodhull, Victoria Claflin (1838–1927) American social reformer" (#PEO160 CP011 037).

Library of Congress: p. 1 "Antietam, Md. Bodies of Confederate dead gathered for burial" (LC-DIG-cwpb-01094); **p. 2** "Beaufort, South Carolina. Group of Negroes on J. J. Smith's Plantation" (#LC-USZ62-67819); **p. 2** "Charleston, South Carolina. Ruins" (LC-DIG-cwpb-02394); **p. 12** "General U. S. Grant, three-quarter-length portrait, standing, facing right, in uniform" (LC-USZ62-1770); **p. 12** "John Wilkes Booth" (LC-USZ62-25166); **p. 16** "Atlanta, Ga. Ruins of depot, blown up on Sherman's departure" (LC-DIG-cwpb-02226); **p. 18** "Richmond ladies going to receive government rations" (LC-USZ62-116427); **p. 21** "The Freedmen's village, Hampton, Virginia" (LC-USZ62-106104); **p. 22** "Selling a freedman to pay his fine, at Monticello, Florida" (LC-USZ62-117139); **p. 28** "Panoramic view of Washington City from the new dome of the Capitol, looking east" (LC-USZ62-64266); **p. 42** "Brig. Maj. Gen. Rufus Saxton" (LC-DIG-cwpb-06589); **p. 52** "The new military commanders in the [in]surrectionary states" (LC-USZ62-127611); **p. 69** "Trumbull, Hon. Lyman of Ill." (LC-DIG-cwpbh-04464); **p. 75** "National Union Republican candidates" (LC-USZ62-7602); **p. 76** "Cover of campaign song 'White Man's Banner'" (LC-USZ62-89310); **p. 77** "Representative Women" (LC-USZ62-5535); **p. 83** "The Fifteenth Amendment and Its Results" (LC-USZ62-22396); **p. 85** "Two members of the Ku Klux Klan in their disguises" (LC-USZ62-119565); **p. 90** "Pinchback, Gov. of La." (LC-DIG-cwpbh-03863); **p. 94** "The Louisiana Murders—Gathering the dead and wounded" (LC-USZ62-111154); **p. 96** "The red flag in New York—riotous communist workingmen driven from Tompkins Square by the mounted police" (LC-USZ62-111180); **p. 97** detail from "The shackle broken—by the genius of freedom" (LC-USZ62-2247); **p. 99** "The First Colored Senator and Representatives" (LC-USZ62-2814); **p. 102** "Hon. Adelbert Ames of Miss." (LC-DIG-cwpbh-00604); **p. 103** "Cartoon showing Ulysses S. Grant as an acrobat, on trapeze 'third term,' holding on to 'whiskey ring' and 'Navy ring,' with strap 'corruption' in his mouth, holding up other acrobats, Shepard, George M. Robeson, William W. Belknap, Murphy, Williams, and Orville E. Babcock" (LC-USZC4-5606); **p. 107** "The Last Stand" (LC-USZ62-89878).

p. 7 1861 map by Kayley LeFaiver.

National Archives: p. 11 freedman's possessory note for 40 acres (RG: 105 E.650 9W4 10/13/2 BX 19, Desc: Cert. of Land Warr. To Freedman Savan. GA, Peter Lloyd Sept. 6, 1865); **p. 31** U.S. Constitution; **p. 101** Ann Blue's savings book (Record Group 101, Records of the Office of the Comptroller of the Currency, Letters Received by the Commissioners of the Freedman's Savings and Trust Company, Box 15, Stack 550, Row 62, Compartment 21, Shelf 06.)

National Humanities Center, Research Triangle Park, North Carolina: p. 26 scan of Equal Suffrage. Address from the Colored Citizens of Norfolk, Va., to the People of the United States, 1865.

New York Public Library: p. 15 Photographs and Prints Division, Schomburg Center for Research in Black Culture, The New York Public Library, Astor, Lenox and Tilden Foundations (SC-CN-98-0221/"Slavery—Branding & Flogging. Furrowed and scarred back of Gordon, a slave who escaped from his master in Mississippi, 1863"); **p. 57** Picture Collection, The Branch Libraries, The New York Public Library, Astor, Lenox and Tilden Foundations (#812942/The State Convention at Richmond, Va., in session.); **p. 61** Picture Collection, The Branch Libraries, The New York Public Library, Astor, Lenox and Tilden Foundations (#807148/"The capture of a freight train of the Union Pacific Railroad by Sioux Indians."); **p. 73** Manuscripts, Archives and Rare Books Division, Schomburg Center for Research in Black Culture, The New York Public Library, Astor, Lenox and Tilden Foundations (SC Rare C 81-16. Tunis G. Campbell. *Hotel Keepers, Head Waiters, and Housekeepers Guide*. Boston, 1848. Frontispiece).

Ohio Historical Society: p. 25 "Martin Robison Delany (1812–1885)."

South Caroliniana Library, University of South Carolina, Columbia: p. 58 William James Whipper, carte-de-visite, by Wearn & Hix, Columbia, S.C. (1924.33).

Special Collections, Howard-Tilton Memorial Library, Tulane University: p. 55 front page of June 2, 1866, issue of the *New Orleans Tribune*.

ACKNOWLEDGMENTS

I am so grateful to Erin Clarke, my steadfast, probing gem of an editor, whose enthusiasm for this book never flagged; Nancy Hinkel, publishing director of Alfred A. Knopf and Crown Books for Young Readers, who championed this book when it was but a dream; Allison Wortche, who was so gracious about how terrible I am with colored pencil; Kate Gartner, who devised (once again!) a dynamite design, cover to cover. Thanks are also due to others in the Random House family for matchless production and post-production work: Anjulee Alvares, Artie Bennett, Terry Borzumato, Godwin Chu, Lisa Goffredi, Jenny Golub, Alison Kolani, Jack Lienke, Liz Rhynerson, Christine Vargas, and Adrienne Waintraub.

This book also had the benefit of other sterling minds and generous souls outside the Random House family: people who read *Cause* at various stages and gave sound feedback. Thank you: Rowland Martin, Jr. (extra thanks for helping me process so much legalese!); Judy Dothard Simmons, writer and editor of Anniston, Alabama, great-great-granddaughter of George Downing (extra thanks for helping me see the forest when I was overwhelmed by the trees and for all the great edits); Marsha Weinstein of Louisville, Kentucky, president of that city's chapter of the League of Women Voters (and no relation to that Louisville "rebel she"); Daryl Michael Scott, professor of U.S. history at Howard University and member of the Executive Council of the Association for the Study of African American Life and History; William Jelani Cobb, assistant professor of history at Spelman College; and Nelta Brunson Gallemore, my sister, who journeyed with me on this project from the first scribbling through the last pass, listened to me babble about all that I could not fit into the book, and did not need to be told which passages were composed through tears.

Procuring visuals and permission to reproduce them can sometimes be a nightmare. Not here! Thanks to: Tom Lisanti and Antony M. Toussaint with the New York Public Library; Beth Bilderback with the South Caroliniana Library, University of South Carolina; Marianne D. Wason with the National Humanities Center; Wayne T. De Cesar and Dennis Michael Edelin with the National Archives; Allen Reuben and Eva Tucholka with Culver Pictures; Leon C. Miller with Tulane University; and Melissa Smith, also with Tulane, who not only helped me identify a right issue of the *New Orleans Tribune* but also gave me a mini-course on the newspaper's history.

For all these blessings and the strength, I thank the Blessed Trinity.

Page numbers in *italics* refer to illustrations.

A

Adams, Dock, *106*
Alaska purchase, 59, 60
American Anti-Slavery Society, *35*, 47, 78
American Equal Rights Association
    (AERA), 77, *77*
American Missionary Association, *24*
American Woman Suffrage Association,
    77–78
Ames, Adelbert, 102, *102*
Anderson, Jourdon, 20, 21
Anderson, P. H., 20, 21
Andersonville prison, *17, 42*
Anthony, Henry, 67–8
Anthony, Susan Brownlow, 77, *77, 78*, 91,
    91, 92, 105
Antietam, Battle of, *1, 23*
Apache-Comanche-Kiowa confederation, *59*
Arapaho-Cheyenne confederation, *59*
Armstrong, Samuel Chapman, *21, 24*
Articles of Confederation, *31*
Atzerodt, George, *19*
Avery, Moses, 55

B

Babcock, Orville, *103*
Baldwin, James, 119
Bannister, Edward Mitchell, *104*
Barton, Clara, 42, *43*
Bell, Alexander Graham, 105
Benjamin, Judah Philip, 6
Berry, Lawrence, *54*
Bingham, John Armor, *42, 67*
black codes, 23, 26, 37
Blackwell, Elizabeth and Emily, *91*
Blackwell, Henry, *91*
Blair, Francis Preston, Jr., *76, 76*
Blue, Ann, *101*
Bond, Hugh Lenox, 83
Booth, John Wilkes, 4–5, 11, 12–3, *12*,

16–7, *19, 42*
Boseman, Benjamin, 57
Boutwell, George Sewall, *42*, 44–5, 67, 80
Bowles, John, 63
Brooks, Preston, 98
Brown, John, 83
Brown v. Board of Education, 120
Bullock, Rufus, 82
Bureau of Refugees, Freedmen, and
    Abandoned Lands, *see* Freedmen's
    Bureau
Butler, Andrew, 98
Butler, Benjamin Franklin, *67, 102*, 109

C

Campbell, Tunis G., Sr. *73*
Camp Sumter, *17*
Capitol Building, U.S., 10, *17*, 22, *28*, 36,
    74, 114
Centennial Exposition, 104–5, *104*, 107
Central Pacific Railroad Company, 34, 60,
    78
Chase, Salmon, 67–8
Child, Lydia Maria, *77*
Civil Rights Act of 1866, 37, 69
Civil Rights Act of 1875, 102, 119–20
Civil Rights Act of 1964, 120
Civil War, U.S., 1, *1*, *2*, 6–7, 8–11, *12,
    14, 15, 16*, 24, 29, 34, *39, 77, 78*,
    90, 110, 117
    see also specific battles
Claflin, Tennessee, 89
Colby, Abram, 56–7, 71, 73, 81–2, 89
Cold Harbor, Battle of, *14*
Colfax, Schuyler, *75, 76*, 103
Colfax massacre, 93–4, *94*, 100, 108
Colored National Labor Union (CNLU), 81
Colt, Elizabeth, 93
Confederate Army, *1, 14, 19*, 23, 41, 47,
    48, 85
Confederate States of America (CSA), 5,
    6–7, *6, 7*, 8–9, 11, *14, 16*, 20, 27, 28–9,
    36, 38, 39, 42, 47, 51–3, 82, 98, 100

Congress, U.S., 9–10, 11, 13, 17, *18*, 22–3, 25, 27, 28–32, *28*, 34, *47*, *56*, 59, 63, 65, 73, *79*, 91, 99, 112, 119
  anti-KKK measures taken by, 86–9
  Johnson's attacks on, 47–8, 51–2, 62, 63, 66
  nation's infrastructure fortified by, 49–50, 112–13
  Reconstruction acts passed by, 49, 51–3, *56*, 71, *75*
  rights of free blacks and, 31–2, 35, 36–8, 45, *50*, 55, 76, 86, 97–100, 102
  Southern representation debate in, 9, *18*, 28–31, 32, 36, 45, 47, *73*,109
  see also House of Representatives, U.S.; Joint Committee on Reconstruction; Senate, U.S.
Congressional Reconstruction, 50–3, *62*, 71, *75*, *76*, 87, 89
  black political gains during, 50–2, 54–8, *57*
  Johnson's opposition to, 51–2, 61–3, 66, 71
Constitution, U.S., 2, 5, 9, *28*, *28*, 29–30, *31*, 36, 37, 52, 54, 64, 65, 102, 107, 112
  see also specific amendments
Corliss, George, 105
Coushatta massacre, 100, 101
Cox, Samuel, 46
Crazy Horse, *107*
Crédit Mobilier scandal, 103
Cresap, Edward Otho, *52*
Crosby, Peter, 100
Custer, George Armstrong, 106, *107*

D

Davis, Henry Winter, *18*
Davis, Jefferson F., 5, 6, *6*, *7*, 16, 17, 29, 47, 53, 65, *83*, 84
Declaration of Independence, 76, 104–5, 119

Delany, Martin Robison, *25*, 58, *58*
DeLarge, Robert Carlos, 99
Democratic Party, 5, 10, 29, *30*, 62, 76, *76*, 89, 90, 101, 120
  in election of 1876, 109–10, 112–13
Dickinson, Anna Elizabeth, *35*, *77*, 92
Douglass, Frederick, 11, 35–6, *35*, *58*, 76–7, *78*, *83*, 89, 100, 109–10
Douglass, Lewis, 35, 81
Downing, George, 35, 36, 58, 81, 100
Dred Scott decision, 2
Du Bois, W.E.B., 24, 32, 120
Dunn, Oscar, 90
Duryee, Abram, 96

E

Electoral Commission, 112, 113, *114*
Elliott, Robert Brown, 56, 89, 97–8, *97*, 99, 100
Emancipation Proclamation, 8–9, *8*, *9*, 11, *25*, 41, 76, *83*

F

Fair Oaks, Battle of, *23*
Farnsworth, John, 87
Fessenden, William, *42*
Fifteenth Amendment, 76–7, *78*, 82, *83*, 86, 98, 108, 119
First Reconstruction Act, 52, *75*
Fish, Hamilton, 82
Fisk, Jim, 80
Foner, Eric, 94, 108, 119
Forrest, Nathan Bedford, 7, 47, 48
Fort Pillow massacre, 48
Fort Sumter, Battle of, 5, 6
Fourteenth Amendment, 37–8, 47, 51, 62, 70–3, 76, *76*, 81, 82, 86, 91, 98, 99, 107, 120
Frank Leslie's Illustrated Newspaper, 22, 57, *61*, *68*, 96, *118*

Freedman's Bank, 96, 100, *101*
Freedmen's Bureau, 23–6, *23*, *24*, *25*, 36–7, 40–2, *42*, 45, *49*, 69, *73*, 100, 109
Furst, A. B., *113*

G

Gettysburg, Battle of, *23*
Gibbs, Jonathan, 57, 89
Gibbs, Mifflin, 57
Gould, Jay, 80
Granger, Gordon, 83
Grant, Ulysses S., *10*, 11, *12*, *52*, 61, 65, 80, 89, 90, 103, *103*, 112, 113, *114*
    anti–Southern violence measures taken by, 86–9, 100–3
    elections of, 75–6, *75*, *76*, 89–90
Great Chicago Fire, 87, *87*
Great Strike, 115–17, *117*
Greeley, Horace, *33*, 65, 89
Greenwood, Grace, *77*, 93

H

Hamburg massacre, 105–6, *106*, 109
Hamlin, Hannibal, 9
Harper, Frances Ellen Watkins, 58, 77, *78*
Harper's Weekly, 9, 15, 17, 18, 21, 24, 38, 39, 44, 46, 49, 50, 52, 54, 56, 64, 66, 74, 79, 80, 85, 88, *88*, 89, 92, 94, *104*, *106*, 107, 108, *113*, *114*, 115, *115*, *116*, *117*
Hayes, Rutherford B., 63, 109, 110, *111*, 112–5, *114*
Hendricks, Thomas, 68, 109
Herold, David, *19*
Higginson, Thomas Wentworth, *91*
High Court of Impeachment, 67–9, *68*
Holden, William, 18–9
House of Representatives, U.S., *5*, 5, 8, 28, *28*, 29, 30, *30*, 32, 35, 42, 49, 71, 75, 82, 87, 97, 98–9, 100

Johnson's impeachment and, 65, 66, *66*, *67*
    see also Congress, U.S.
Houzeau, Jean-Charles, 55
Howard, Jacob, *42*
Howard, Oliver Otis, *23*, 24–6, 49
Howard University, 49, 51
Howe, Julia Ward, *91*

I

immigrants, 34, 36, 60–1, *62*, 76, 117, 119
Ingersoll, Roger, 110
Iola Leroy; Or, Shadows Uplifted (Harper), 78

J

James, Jesse, *34*, 106–7
Johnson, Andrew, 4–5, 6–7, 9, 10–11, *12*, 16–20, *19*, 29, *42*, 47, 50, *50*, 51, 52, 73, 82, 102, 117
    attacks on Congress by, 47–8, 51–2, 62, 63, 66
    black delegation meeting with, 35–6, 58
    civil rights and pro-black bills vetoed by, 36–8, 45
    Congressional Reconstruction opposed by, 51–2, 61–3, 66, 70–1
    impeachment trial of, 64–9, *66*, *67*, *70*, 70–1, 76, 89
    Lincoln's assassination and, 4, 13, 17
    racist views of, 11, 21–2, 23, 31, 36, 37–8, 47, *50*, 52, 62, 63
    reconfiscation order of, 25–7
    see also Presidential Reconstruction
Johnson, Lyndon Baines, 120
Johnson, Reverdy, *42*, 86
Joint Committee on Reconstruction, 28–9, 37, 39, 42, *42*, 44–5
    see also Reconstruction

K

Kellogg, William, 90, 93
Key, Philip Barton, 62
Ku Klux Klan (KKK), 47, 48, 53, 71, 81,
    85, 86–9, 99, 109
Ku Klux Klan Act, 86, 87

L

Lawrence, William, 29
Lee, Richard Henry, 105
Lee, Robert E., 11, 35, 84
Lewis, Edmonia, 104
Life and Public Services of Martin R. Delany
    (Rollin), 58, 58
Lincoln, Abraham, 7, 8, 11–12, 12, 18,
    27, 41, 42, 66, 110
  assassination of, 4–5, 12–3, 12, 16, 19,
    31
  elections of, 6, 9–11
  Emancipation Proclamation of, 8–9, 9,
    11
  Proclamation of Amnesty and
    Reconstruction of, 9, 18
  Ten Percent Plan of, 9, 12, 46
Lippincott, Sara Jane Clarke, 77
Livermore, Mary Ashton Rice, 77
Logen, John Alexander, 67
Long, Jefferson Franklin, 99
*Lost Cause, The: A New Southern History
    of the War of the Confederates*, 53
Lynch, James, 55

M

Mallory, Stephen Russell, 6
March to the Sea, 23
Marvin, William, 20
Marx, Karl, 67
McClellan, George, 10
Memminger, Christopher Gustavus, 6
Memphis riot, 38, 109

Monroe, John, 46
Mott, Lucretia, 77
Moulton, Samuel, 29
Myers, Isaac, 81
Mystery, The, 25

N

Nast, Thomas, 46, 50, 106
National Association for the
    Advancement of Colored People
    (NAACP), 120
National Labor Union (NLU), 80–1
National Woman Suffrage Association, 77
Native Americans, 3, 7, 21, 34, 37, 59,
    60, 60, 61, 78, 79, 93, 104, 106,
    107, 113, 119
New Orleans riot, 46, 46, 109
New Orleans Tribune, 55, 55
New York Day-Book, 45
New York Stock Exchange, 95, 95
New York Times, 16, 38, 78, 110, 112
New York Tribune, 18, 89, 112
Nobel, Alfred, 61
North Carolina Proclamation, 18–20
North Star, 25

O

Oates, William, 14

P

Pacific Railroad, 33–4, 33, 60, 79, 95
Panic of 1873, 95–6, 95
Parker, Ely, 37
Peck, John, 76
Pendleton, George, 10
Perry, Benjamin, 31
Phillips, Wendell, 47
Pinchback, Pinckney Benton Stewart, 90,
    90
Planters' Banner, 74

Plessy v. Ferguson, 120
Pope, John, *52*
Powell, Lewis, *19*
Presidential Reconstruction, 19–20
    as antagonistic to black advancement, 21, 25–7
    Republicans' opposition to, 22–3, 25–7, 48
Proclamation of Amnesty and Reconstruction, 9, 18
Providence Evening Press, 35, 36

R

Rainey, Joseph Hayne, 99, *99*
Raymond, Henry, 29
Reagan, John Henninger, 6
"rebel shes," 16, *18*
Reconstruction, 1–3, 9, 13, 119–21
    education of blacks in, *2*, *21*, *24*, *49*, *57*, 120
    Native American relocation and, 3, 34, 59–60, *60*, 93, 106, 113, 119
    railroad expansion during, 33–4, 60–1, 78–9, *79*, 94–5
    Republicans gain control of, 50–1
    worker conflict and unemployment in, 80–1, 96, *96*, 115–17, *115*, *116*, *117*
    see also Congressional Reconstruction; Presidential Reconstruction
"Redeemers," 100, 102, *106*
Republican Party, 6, 10, 25, *25*, 30, 51, 66, 69, 75, *75*, 76, 81, 88, 89, 97, 120
    Congressional Reconstruction and, 50–1, *75*, 97
    in election of 1876, 102–3, 109–10, 112–15
    Presidential Reconstruction opposed by, 22–3, 25–6, 27, 47
Revels, Hiram Rhoades, 83, 99
Robeson, George, *103*
Rollin, Frances, 58, *58*
Ruby, George, 56

S

Saxton, Rufus, *11*, 42–3, *42*
Schofield, John McAllister, *52*
Scott, Robert, 86
Second Reconstruction Act, 52
Senate, U.S., 5, *5*, *18*, 28, *28*, 30, 32, 51, 61, 71, 82, 83, 98, *98*, 100, 101, 102, 109
    Johnson's impeachment trial in, 65, 66–9, *69*
    see also Congress, U.S.
Seneca Falls convention, *35*, *77*
Seward, William Henry, 4, 16, *19*, 31, 60, 71
Seymour, Horatio, 76, *76*
sharecropping, 39
Shellabarger, Samuel, 63
Sheridan, Philip Henry, 10, 46, 52, *52*, 61–2, *61*, 65, 87, 101
Sherman, William Tecumseh "Cump," 10, *10*, *16*, 23, 25, 26, *31*, 34, 73, 113
Sickles, Daniel Edgar, *52*, 62, *62*, 65
Sitting Bull, *107*
"Slabtown," *21*
Slaughterhouse Cases, 107
slavery, 1–2, *2*, 5, *5*, 8, 13, 14–15, 20, 24, 25, 27, 29, 30, 35, *35*, 36, 56, 57, 67, 73, 78, 83, 93, *93*, 97, 98, 108, 110
    abolishment of, 6, *7*, 8–9, *9*, 30–2, 76, 77, 89
    reparations and, 1, 32, 53
Smith, Amanda Berry, 93, *93*
Special Field Order No. 15, *10*, *11*, 25, *73*
Stanton, Edwin McMasters, 10, 16, 29, 42, 51, 61, *62*, 64, 65, 66, 69, 77
Stanton, Elizabeth Cady, *35*, 76, 77, *77*, *78*, 105
Stephens, Alexander, 27, 84
Stevens, Thaddeus, 10, 11, 22, 26, 29–32, *30*, 39, *42*, 47, 49, 52–3, 63, 65–6, 67, 69, 71, 73, *74*, 109
Stone, Lucy, 77, *78*, 91

Sumner, Charles, 65, 68, 98, 98, 99, 100, 101–2, 109
Supreme Court, U.S., 2, 67, 107–8, 112, 114, 119–20
Surratt, Mary, 19, 42

T

Taney, Roger, 2–3
Tarbell, John, 44–5
Tashunca-Uitco (Crazy Horse), 107
Tatanka-Iyotanka (Sitting Bull), 107
Taylor, Richard, 53
Ten Percent Plan, 9, 12, 46
Tenth Amendment, 5
Tenure of Office Act, 51, 61, 65, 66
Third Reconstruction Act, 52
Thirteenth Amendment, 9–10, 11, 13, 19, 27, 31, 35, 98
Thomas, George Henry, 52
Thompson, Sarah, 99–100
Throckmorton, James, 61–2
Tilden, Samuel, 109, 110, 112
Toombs, Robert, 6
Trefousse, Hans, 119
Trumbull, Lyman, 68, 69
Turner, Benjamin Sterling, 99
Twain, Mark, 33, 103
Tweed, William Magear "Boss," 109, 109
Twitchell, Marshall, 100

U

Union Army, 2, 7, 8, 9, 9, 11, 12, 14, 15, 16, 25, 35, 42, 42, 43, 48, 53, 57, 58, 76, 83, 90, 96, 110
Union League, 54, 56, 99
Union Navy, 29, 55
Union Pacific Railroad Company, 34, 61, 78, 103
U.S. v. Cruikshank, 108
U.S. v. Reese, 108

V

Vanderbilt, Cornelius, 65, 81, 89
Vickers, George, 68–9

W

Wade, Benjamin Franklin, 16, 18, 21, 66–7, 75, 109
Waite, Morrison, 108, 114
Waldron, Adelia, 61
Walker, Leroy Pope, 6
Walla Walla Statesman, 86
Walls, Thomas, 99
Warmoth, Henry, 90
Washburne, Elihu, 42, 69
Washington, Booker Taliaferro, 24
Waud, Alfred, 44, 56
Welles, Gideon, 29, 29
Wells, James, 46
Wells-Barnett, Ida, 120
Westbrook, Betsey, 89
Wheeler, William, 109
Whipper, William, 35, 58
Whipper, William James, 58
White League, 93, 100
White Man's Party, 100–1
Wilder, L. Douglas, 90
Williams, George, 42, 103
Williams, Thomas, 67
Wilson, Henry, 103
Wilson, James Falconer, 67
Wirz, Hartmann Heinrich "Henry," 17
Woman's Declaration of Rights and Sentiments, 35
Woman's Journal, 91–3, 91
women's rights, 3, 12, 35, 58, 66, 73, 76–8, 79, 89, 91–3, 104, 105, 119, 120
Woodhull, Victoria Claflin, 89–90, 89
workmen's riots, 115–17, 116, 117